THREE

Sulby Johnstone

SERMONS,

ON THE SUBJECT OF

SCRIPTURE POLITICS.

By the Rev. W. S. DICKSON, D. D.

BELFAST:

PRINTED IN THE YEAR 1793.

PREFACE.

IN the following sheets, the reader is not to expect any of the characters of a laboured production. The circumstance which forced them on the public eye, must render such expectation vain. This was the unqualified assertion that, their contents were " *Sedition, Treason, Popery.*"

How far the assertion is founded in truth, the public are now to judge ; and they may rest assured, that they are laid before them, exactly as preached, without alteration, and without correction. The second and third were, each, the production of three days, before their respective dates, and never underwent the polish of a second copying.

The first was written, at an early period of the Author's life, and preached before the general Synod of Ulster, in June 1781. Since that time it has not undergone the alteration of a single word. This circumstance, is mentioned to shew that the liberal sentiments of the Presbyterians, towards their Catholic brethren, are not the hot-bed plants of the moment, as has been invidiously represented. They have been the sentiments of the Author these twenty years. And from the favorable reception which this Sermon met in 1781, he thinks himself justified in saying, they were then the sentiments of his Rev. Fathers and brethren. It was preached in the congregation of of Portaferry, word for word, as it is printed, (the concluding address accepted) on the Sunday before Christmas last. But as this address was part of what was delivered before the Synod, it is now printed with it,

This is the second time which the Author has been obliged to expose his abortive offspring to the world, by the ignorance or malice of wicked men. To the former attempt to calumniate and deſtroy him, he owes the origin of what little reputation the partiality of the public has allowed him. What may be the iſſue of the preſent, reſts with the ſame tribunal. He adds, that whatever conſtruction may be put on his words, there is not a heart in his Majeſty's dominions more warmly attached to his real intereſts, or the principles of the Britiſh conſtitution, than the heart which dictated the following ſentiments; and that the warmth with which he has occaſionally mentioned Catholic e-mancipation, and reform, aroſe, not merely from the principles of juſtice and humanity, but from the full conviction, that as the happineſs of our King muſt be inſeparable from that of his people, ſo their union among themſelves, and attachment to his perſon and government, founded on equality of right, privilege, and protection, according to the original principles of the conſtitution, form the only ſolid baſe on which that happineſs and his throne can reſt ſecure.

He is aware, that many apologies ought to be made for troubling the public with the concerns of an individual, or the calumnies to which he may be expoſed. Theſe, however, he ſhall leave to the good nature of his countrymen, whoſe indulgence hitherto, has far exceeded his deſervings. And if the following ſheets ſhall be the means of conveying, or confirming one juſt idea, or liberal ſentiment; or in any manner promoting the dignity, peace, and proſperity of his countrymen, he will rejoice in the calumnies which have been uttered againſt him, while he prays for the reformation and forgiveneſs of their Authors.

Portaferry, February 1793.

THREE

SERMONS,

ON THE SUBJECT OF

SCRIPTURE POLITICS.

JOHN, chap. 18. verse 26. " *My Kingdom is not of this World.*"

THE extraordinary power displayed in the miracles of Jesus, and the benevolence with which it was exercised, seem to have produced a general disposition to receive him, as the great deliverer, which prophecy had foretold to the people of Israel. And when they saw him raising the dead, and feeding multitudes in the Wilderness with a few loaves and small fishes, they concluded that, as he could thus easily support armies, and rescue the slain from

the hand of death, he would realize the hopes of temporal dominion, with which they had been long intoxicated, and urged him
to affume the title of King.

As this overture was founded on miftaken apprehenfions of his
kingdom, inftead of compliance, he endeavoured to correct the
prejudices from which it proceeded, and the paffions connected
with them. But they were fo firmly attached to the hopes, which
ambition and revenge had long cherifhed, that they were offended ;
turned that refentment againft him, of which they had attempted
to make him the inftrument ; joined iffue with his enemies in a
fcandalous profecution, and obliged the Governor of Judæa to
confent to his death.

The moft remarkable circumftance in this tranfaction, is that
on which they founded their accufations. They charged him
with the feditious defigns, in which they had laboured in vain to
engage him ; and, as they pretended, they brought their charge,
merely becaufe his claims were unfriendly to Cæfar.——That Cæfar,
whofe claims they wifhed to fhake off ; in overthrowing whofe
empire they would have gloried, and in oppofition to whom, they
had endeavoured, by compulfion, to make him a King.

The Roman Governor, before whom the charge was exhibited,
was aware of the bafe motives on which it was urged, and fully
fatisfied of the innocence of Jefus. He knew, that through
envy they had delivered him up ; yet he feems to have fufpected
that fome of his claims might have been expreffed in terms which
might juftify the conftruction which had been put upon them.
Perhaps he had connected fome of the extravagant epithets which
the ftoic philofophy beftowed upon its wife man, with the ideas of
that exalted wifdom which Jefus taught ; and imagined that, in
fuch a fenfe, he had arrogated to himfelf the name of King. Be
this as it may, he defired to know whether, in any fenfe, he affum-
ed this title, and what that fenfe was.

To Pilate's inquiries on this fubject, Jefus admitted, in anfwer, that he was a King ; but informed him that his claims, as
fuch, did not interfere with thofe of the Emperor, from whom
Pilate derived his authority, and to whom he owed allegiance ;
and added a circumftance from which he might be affured that
this information was true.

" My Kingdom is not of this World ; if my kingdom were of this world, then would my fervants fight, that I might not be delivered to the Jews ; but now, is my Kingdom not from hence."

Whatever ideas Pilate entertained of the kingdom of Jefus, from this declaration it is evident that he did not imagine there was any interference between it and the interefts of Cæfar ; or that his loyalty could be impeached on account of the lenity with which he treated him : for he immediately went out and declared publicly, that he found " * in him no fault at all."

However favourable this may appear to the character and pretenfions of Jefus, no fatisfying argument can be deduced from it in favour of chriftianity. Pilate had no fixed principles, nor any clear views of it, to enable him to pronounce upon its merits. The only obvious conclufion was that which he formed, by connecting the idea of " Kingdom" with that of " bearing witnefs to the truth," that a man who profeffed only to teach and fupport truth, and acted agreeably to his profeffion, could not be an enemy to good government, or the interefts of fociety.

Yet many inquieries remain concerning truth in general, and particularly, concerning chriftianity as teaching the truth, or exhibiting juft views of the various and important fubjects of which it treats. But as it would be impoffible to comprife them all in the bounds of a Sermon, we fhall confine our attention at prefent to one which arifes directly from the declaration before us.

Previous to the difcuffion of this inquiry, it may not be improper to afcertain the meaning of the declaration itfelf.

" This World," from its inordinate influence on the paffions and conduct of men, is often contrafted with " the Father," who is the fource of all good ; and from the diftreffes in which the immoderate love of it involves them to " Heaven," which is the feat of perfect happinefs. Hence, thofe who devote themfelves principally to the indulgence of appetite, are faid to be " of the World ;" whilft thofe who cherifh more exalted fentiments, and purfue the more valuable attainments of wifdom, truth, and virtue, are denominated " of the Father." Thus Chrift addreffed

* John 18. 38.

the Jews; prejudices and worldly attachments rendered them blind to the purposes of Heaven: " * Ye are from beneath, I am from above: Ye are of this world, I am not of this world." In the same sense he used the phrases frequently in his discourses to, and concerning his disciples: " † Because ye are not of the world, but I have chosen you out of the world, therefore the world hateth you." Again, " ‡ I have given them thy word, and the world hath hated them, because they are not of the world, even as I am not of the world."

These passages shew that, " to be of the world," is to adopt the designs, indulge the passions, or engage in the pursuits which center in it. And to be " not of the world," is to be free from their destructive influence.

In this sense the phrase applies as strictly to collective bodies as to individuals. They also take their characters from the ends which they have in view, and the means by which they propose to accomplish them. The character, therefore, which is here given of christianity, may be comprehended under the following particulars:

I. It did not originate from worldly policy.

II. It doth not affect pomp, magnificence, and perishable wealth, which flatter the vanity, and gratify the ambition and avarice of men.

III. It disclaims every idea of being extended by violence, or supported by oppression. And,

IV. It exercises no dominion over men but what truth and righteousness fully justify, and the reason of its subjects must ever approve and rejoice in.

These characters of the Messiah's kingdom admit of an easy and clear illustration. They are strongly marked in the prophetic writings; in the declarations and conduct of Jesus, and the Ministrations of the Apostles, by whom its influence was extended. They lead us to the original and proper idea of it, as founded in

---

* John 8, 23.　　　　† 15, 19.　　　　‡ 17, 14.

truth and righteousness, having its seat in the hearts of men, consisting in goodness, gentleness, and peace; aud supported by its own intrinsic excellence, and the powerful attestations which prove that " it is of the Father."

But though christianity is a system purely moral and religious—though it is not marked with the characters of human policy, nor dependent on it ; we are not to conclude that it bears no relation to civil government, or is unconcerned in the laws by which it is regulated. This would be a conclusion, rash, unwarranted, and dangerous. It would at once remove the strongest barrier which ever hath been, or ever can be opposed to the passions of men.

We shall, therefore, enquire how far, and in what manner the kingdom of Christ is, or ought to be connected with the kingdoms of the world; or in other words, how far, and in what manner, religion and politics are related.

In this inquiry, the kingdom of Jesus is to be considered as a system of pure and universal morality, enforced from religious considerations. That this system hath man as its object, and in all parts tends to his improvement and happiness, will not be denied in this place. We may add too, that it respects him in every relation in which he may be placed, as this is necessarily implied in the idea of universal morality.

This morality, which is the great object of religion, and ought to be the basis of all government, is in itself unchangeable ; and under whatever form it hath been exhibited, or motives enforced in the different stages of civilization, is intrinsically the same.

Should this remark be thought to require any illustration, Revelation amply supplies it. We can hardly conceive of any systems more widely different, in many particulars, than the two which form its principal contents. The one is calculated for a particular people, proposes to keep them distinct from all the nations of the earth, is loaded with rites and ceremonies, and confines its prospects to the present life. The other presents itself to all mankind, proposes to abolish distinctions in respect to religious privileges, and unite the whole in one great family ; is divested of the artificial aid of ritual observance, and brings forward all the treasures of immortality to enrich its votaries, and its horrors to appal the spirit of iniquity. Yet with all this difference of circumſtance and motive, the morality of both is exactly the ſame. "Thou ſhalt love the Lord thy God, with all thy heart, with all thou ſoul, with all thy ſtrength, and with all thy mind, and thy neighbour as thy ſelf."

As theſe general precepts comprehend the ſum of human duty, they expreſs the principles by which it ſhould be regulated, and are the great objects of both ſyſtems.

In the latter of theſe precepts, it is taken for granted, that men are uniformly induced with the principle of ſelf-love, in a degree ſufficient to impel them to the purſuit of happineſs. And as this principle is the ſtandard by which the love of others is to be regulated, the leaſt which can be inferred is, that thoſe who acknowledge the authority of the precepts, ſhould ſo far cheriſh the benevolent affections, as is neceſſary to engage them in promoting and ſecuring the happineſs of others. With this inference the deſcriptions of the love enjoined in the goſpel, and the effects which it ought to produce, are perfectly conformable. It reſtrains from injury, diſdains the narrow limits of religious or political aſſociations, and riſes ſuperior to enmity and inſult. "* Love worketh no ill to his neighbour; ſuffereth long and is kind; envieth not; rejoiceth not in iniquity, but rejoiceth in the truth." Nor are the claims of chriſtianity ſatisfied by that indolent complacency which expreſſeth itſelf, only in unavailing wiſhes of proſperity, or fair profeſſions of good-will. The love which it enjoins muſt preſs forward into action; ſet oppoſition and dangers at defiance; and if the public good requires, bravely encounter death itſelf. "† Let us not love in word, nor in tongue, ſaith the Apoſtle, but in deed and in truth." "‡ To do good, and to communicate, forget not; for with ſuch ſacrifices God is well pleaſed." And ſaith Jeſus, "This is my commandment, that ye love one another, even as I have loved you." "Love your enemies, bleſs them who curſe you, do good to them who hate you, and pray for them who deſpitefully uſe you."

From theſe expreſſions we perceive that as chriſtianity inculcates the generous affections, the happineſs of man is the great end which it propoſes, to which it directs his activity, and to the promotion of which it lends its ſolemn ſanctions. And the more any

* Rom. 13, 10.   1 Cor. 13. 4, 6.   † 1 John, 3, 10.
‡ Heb. 13, 16.

relation in life affects this happiness, the more important it becomes, and the more immediate object of religious infpection and
religious influence.

Among thefe relations, various and interefting as they are, that
which binds an individual to the ftate of which he is a member, is
the moft important. In it the influence of one may occupy a
wide extended circuit, and materially affect the fecurity and happinefs of many. Nay! the inftances are not infrequent of kingdoms
refcued from the very brink of deftruction, by the wifdom or
prowefs of an individual; while on the other hand, we have feen
empires hurled from the fummit of profperity into the gulph of
confufion, and all their proud trophies buried in ruins, at the feet
of one ambitious mortal. On it the duties of fubordinate relations depend for protection, and from their tendency to raife men to
the exalted character of citizens, much of their importance is derived. This too muft ever vary with the extent of a ftate, as duties and ranks multiply in proportion to its increafe.

However, all this variety of rank is comprehended in the general
divifion of men into magiftrate and fubject, the former of whom
is entrufted with the execution of laws, which the latter have fanctified with their approbation, and to which they are amenable.
The laws which refpect this arrangement, and mark the recipro-
cal duties, of which it lays the foundation, have received the name
of politics, and conftitute a moft interefting branch of morality,
confidered as a fcience.

In the firft ftages of fociety, and in fmall ftates, fubordinate
diftinctions are few. Hence their internal politics are fimple, and
comprifed in fmall bounds. A moderate fhare of prudence and
fagacity, connected with perfonal courage, a fenfe of juftice, and
patience of hardfhip, are fufficient for all the purpofes of counfel
or war. In ordinary circumftances, old age, which is the repofi-
tory of knowledge, and in which experience hath refcued the underftanding from the influence of the more turbulent paffions, holds
the feat of executive juftice; and when external dangers threaten,
or counfels of war prevail, he whofe bravery and patience have
been formerly proved is called forth to command, and the moft im-
plicit refpect is paid to his authority. But as foon as the caufe
for which he is promoted ceafes to operate, his authority expires,

B

and he finks, as before, to a level with his brethren. However, if his exertions are crowned with fuccefs, his tribe is emboldened, new enterprizes are undertaken, and his appointment is renewed ; the fame of his prowefs fpreads around, his alliance is courted, and fear induces a fubmiffion to his arms. Yet, ftill his authority expires with the enterprize for which it was given him.

But though his authority is fhortlived, the effects of it are often permanent. The nations whom his arms have fubdued, or virtues conciliated, unite in one common intereft, and become objects of jealoufy or fear to all their neighbours. Hence combinations are formed to check their growing power, and balance their influence.

Thus ftates proceed from fmall to great ; and in this procefs, the face of things takes a new afpect and complexion. As population increafes, the neceffaries of life come into greater demand. And, as the refources of nature fail, after many ftruggles, art is called in to her affiftance. Hence originates private property ; and the variety of fuccefs which attends the efforts of individuals, in time, lays the foundation of a permanent diftinction in ranks. He who is indolent or unfuccefsful, muft fubmit to him whofe labours have produced more than his wants require : And dependence for bread gives an influence, which is often lafting, and generally increafes, as fuperiority in wealth prevails.

This inequality fupplies new matter to excite and employ the diffocial paffions. Pride demands humiliating expreffions of the dependence which wealth hath created ; ambition afpires to an increafe of power ; whilft poverty, *galled by infult* and *oppreffion,* complains, that power is overftretched ; becomes clamorous and turbulent, and labours to throw off the painful yoke. Hence endlefs difcord is introduced, and in its effects, plainly demonftrates, that fomething more ftable and juft, than the capricious will of an interefted individual, is neceffary to afcertain the rights, regulate the interefts, and fecure the happinefs of men united in fociety.

The conviction of this gives a new turn to human affairs. Laws are eftablifhed as ftandards of right ; and one, or a few, are deputed to give them activity, and regulate their execution. Hence, as government ftands on fixed principles, it takes a regular form ;

and this form is originally modelled by the prevailing taste or ci cumstances of the state.

It appears, in general, that states delegated but a small part of their power at first. A jealousy of their rights induced them to reserve matters of national concern for national debate. Accordingly, in new-born states, war and peace were never determined but in the public assembly of the people. But as population increased, and territories were enlarged, such assemblies became inconvenient, and sometimes impossible, even on the most important occasions. Hence, more extensive delegations were adopted; and the most valuable interests, and solemn deliberations, were intrusted to a few.

These delegations, however well adapted to the purposes for which they were made, seem to have been early perverted. Power is always intoxicating; and whatever the sources or means of power may be, ambition will endeavour to perpetuate and increase it. In these struggles for pre-eminence the more knowing or powerful prevail; success secures friends; and authority is erected on the basis of corruption. Sometimes indeed, the very fear of tyranny creates tyrants; and the apprehension of slavery gives birth to despotism. In the hardy struggles which men make for liberty, some favourite patron is called in, by whose generous efforts the dreaded evils are averted for a season. On such occasions the overflowings of gratitude despise all bounds. An infatuated people throw themselves into the arms of a deliverer, as if he rose superior to human infirmities. But alas! experience soon proves the contrary. He, in turn, is intoxicated with power; he considers unlimated submission as scarcely adequate to his past services; and popular confidence lulls suspicion asleep, 'till he rivets the chains of slavery too fast to be broken without violence and convulsion. In this case, resistance is branded with the name of rebellion; and the complexion of rebellion darkened with the charge of ingratitude.

But in whatever manner these changes are introduced, and power centered in individuals, the event is the same. All governments tend to despotism; and by degrees, more or less rapid, terminate in it.

From all these circumstances, taken together, we see, that the desire of security and peace gave birth to civil societies; and that all the revolutions, in the mode of governing them, have arisen from it. We see too, that all civil authority is originally derived from the people; that no individual hath any right to govern but what they bestow; and, of consequence, that their protection, safety, and happiness are, or *ought to be*, the great ends of government; and the supreme law to which all others should be subordinate.

This doctrine, however ungrateful to ambition, will ever be supported by reason and humanity. The spirit of despotism may counteract, but cannot invalidate, or disapprove it. Indeed it carries its evidence in its own bosom; and in its certainty, brings us to an important point in the present inquiry. It shews us that the end of christianity and good government is the same; and consequently, that in this important particular, religion and politics are inseparably connected.

If this end is the happiness of mankind, as we have endeavoured to shew, we are led from it to a conclusion of great importance. We are obliged to acknowledge, either that this happiness may be attained and secured by means essentially different; or that, in them also, the connexion between religion and politics must be preserved inviolate.

This alternative can never subject us to any difficulty. Experience shews, that virtue alone leads to true happiness: and religion inculcates virtue, as they only mean to promote and secure *it*, and the favour of God, with whom the treasures of it remain. In this view it marks distinctly the duties of every relation, and claims an authority to enforce them. It represents every individual as under the cognizance, and subject to the controul of Heaven: And from the influence which men in authority may have, and ought to use, in the cause of virtue, it speaks of Magistrates, in particular, as the Ministers of God: *i. e.* as servants acting under him in promoting that happiness which is the great end of his administration. When they depart from this character, Revelation charges them with guilt, commands repentence, and points out the measures by which the destructive tendencies of injustice and oppression may be corrected, " * Thus, saith the Lord God; remove violence and spoil; execute judgment and justice;

* Ezek. 5. 9.

take away your exactions from my people." " * Loofe the bands of wickednefs ; undo the heavy burdens ; let the oppreffed go free ; and break every yoke." " † Keep mercy and do judgment ; " ‡ For mercy and truth uphold the King ; his throne is eftablifhed by righteoufnefs." It marks alfo, the popular effects of fuch conduct, and contrafts it with the iffue of licentioufnefs and oppreffion. " ‖ When the righteous is in authority, the people rejoice ; but when the wicked beareth rule, the people mourn."

From the certainty of thefe obfervations, and the many temptations to which magiftracy is expofed, Revelation afferts, that a fenfe of religion is the only principle on which their influence can be counteracted ; and prefcribes it as an indifpenfible quality in men who are to be intrufted with civil power. " § Provide, out of all the people, able men, fuch as fear God, men of truth, hating covetoufnefs :" " ¶ Wife men, and underftanding, known among your tribes, and place fuch to be rulers over you ;" " For he that ruleth over men muft be juft, ruling in the fear of God.*"

There is a circumftance in thefe words, which is too important to be overlooked. While they ftrongly mark the characters of men, who may be fafely intrufted with civil authority, they give a folemn fanction to an obfervation already made. They refolve all authority into the appointment of the people ; and place the rights of choice and inveftiture entirely in them.

But though this be the cafe, we are not to fuppofe that Revelation places the people above the reach of government and law. Every individual owes fubjection to the ftate : and though magiftracy derives its power from the people, it poffeffeth alfo the fanction of divine approbation. To them, who rule with uprightnefs, honor, refpect, and obedience are juftly due, and ftrictly injoined by the word of God. " † Let every foul be fubject to the higher powers ; not only for wrath, but for confcience fake. Render to all their dues, tribute to whom tribute is due, cuftom to whom cuftom, fear to whom fear, honor to whom honor." " ‡ Submit yourfelves to every ordinance of man, for the Lord's fake ; whether it be to the King as fupreme, or unto governors, who are

---

* Ifa. 5. 6. + Hof. 12. 6. ‡ Pro. 20. 28. Ifa. 16. 4.

‖ Prov. 29. 2. § Exod. 18. 21. ¶ Deut. 1. 13.

* 2 Sam. 23. 3. † Rom. 13. 1. 5. 7. ‡ 1. Pet. 2. 13.

sent by him, for the punishment of evil doers, and the praise of them who do well."

The Jewish law consigned those who disobeyed magistrates, in the exercise of their duty, to " * imprisonment, confiscation of goods, banishment, or death," according to the nature of their crimes ; and christianity carries its vengeance still farther ; and declares " † that the Lord knoweth how to reserve the unjust to the day of judgment ; but *chiefly*, those who despise government, and speak evil of dignities." Still, however, religion admits, that disobedience is criminal, *only* when the power of the magistrate is exercised " *for the punishment of evil doers, and the praise of them who do well.*" When this order is inverted, magistracy violates the principle upon which it was established ; every claim to respect and obedience is cancelled ; and resistance becomes, not only lawful, but necessary and honorable. On this principle the midwives of Egypt have immortalized their names ; the army of Saul will be mentioned for ever, in terms peculiarly honorable ; and the name of Daniel will be remembered with reverence, as long as sun and moon endure.

Upon the whole, the kingdom of Christ claims a strict connexion with the kingdoms of the world. It challengeth authority over them, marks distinctly, the duties of every station ; and injoins the performance of them by its solemn sanctions.

Should it be asked, " How far doth this connexion extend ?" what hath been offered on this subject, will help us to a ready answer. It extends to every measure which can affect the persons, reputations, properties, or enjoyments of men. Whatever, therefore, is unfriendly to human happiness or improvement, tends at once to defeat the end of the Gospel, and of good government : And the neglect or abuse of the powers and means by which these may be promoted, argues a want of that spirit, which the former was intended to inspire, and the latter must cherish for its own support.

The only circumstance, relative to government, over which religion does not claim controul, is the form under which it may be administered. It leaves this as matter of perfect indifference, and,

* Ezra. 7. 26.   † 2 Pet. 9. 10.

provided the end of government is accomplished, it allows the taste and circumstances of states to determine, whether their executive powers shall continue in the body at large, be intrusted to a few, or resigned intirely into the hands of an individual.

Having proceeded thus far, it remains to inquire, in what manner religion and politics are connected. However obvious the answer to this inquiry may appear, from what hath been already offered, it seems to have been almost universally mistaken. Though men have seldom denied the reality of this connexion, yet they have arranged the parties connected in an order which reason and the nature of things disclaim, and religion must ever abhor. Though politics is only a part of morality; and though religion comprehends the whole, and gives it energy by her solemn sanctions, yet the part assigned to religion is subordinate to policy, and the dependence to which she hath been reduced, truly humiliating. She hath been shackled by forms of human device, as if the parent of happiness was in danger of destroying her favourite issue; bedizened with ceremonies, as if such taudry ornaments could add to her native beauty; fortified by penal statutes, and guarded by gibbets, racks, and flames, as if the solid arguments, on which she rests her claims, and the power of God,—and the only power which she acknowledges—were not sufficient to protect and support her.

The effects of this arrangement have fully proved that it is not more impious, than it is absurd. *Impious* it is, because God alone is the light of the understanding, and Lord of conscience: And it *must be absurd,* as opinion is independent, even of him who holds it. It owns no influence but that of evidence; and as this may vary, it will continually change. It is *even worse* than absurd. It hath sacrificed religion to appearances—realities to a shadow—by diverting the attention of mankind from the important matters of the law, with which their interests, improvement, and happiness, are inseparably connected; and instead of that mild and gentle spirit, which proclaims glad tidings, and diffuses peace and joy among men, it hath substituted a dæmon which sounds the trump of war, spreads havock and desolation through the world, and deluges the earth with human blood.

The same presumption which hath degraded religion to a slave, and armed her with terrors and death, hath attempted to subject the duty to human policy, and render his power subservient to the passions of men. Examples of this are scarcely noticed in the history of the heathen world. From the extraction and character of their gods they seem perfectly natural. When we reflect that Mercury was a thief, and Venus a prostitute, we cannot be surprised that the one should be invoked in schemes of theft and rapine, and the other of debauchery. And when we consider Jupiter as the usurper of his father's throne, and tyrant of Heaven, we are prepared to see tyrants bow the knee before him, and regale his priests with smoking victims, whilst states invoke his patronage in aid of violence and oppression. Here religion is the natural parent of corruption ; and the grossest enormities take shelter under the example of the gods.

Though the character of the true God is widely different from those of the heathen world, yet we find the same attempts, which we have mentioned, made to interest him in the cause of iniquity. When states have adopted schemes of conquest, whether from avarice, ambition, or revenge, religion is strained hard to justify their execution ; its Ministers are made the echoes of political mandates ; and Heaven's lofty arch resounds with loud invocations to God, that he would divest himself of his excellence, accommodate his will to the passions of men, and bless their attempts to undo his creation, and defeat the designs of his gracious providence.

Whoever thinks seriously, for one moment, will perceive that, as this is an office abhorrent from the nature of God, it is also founded upon a station to which He rises far superior. As He leans not on the feeble authority, He will not stoop to become the pliant tool of human policy, or abject slave to passions which He implanted at first, for wise and good purposes, and hath an absolute right to controul and regulate.

From these things we may conclude, that religion is not connected with politics, as an equal, much less as a dependent. Every argument which proves that God hath a right to govern the world ; and that Revelation comes from God ; proves also, that the principles of Revelation should regulate the counsels and designs of men ; and that human laws can never justify measures, which those of God condemn.

This principle is urged with remarkable strictness under the

Jewiſh diſpenſation. On all important occaſions recourſe was had to the law, before any important deciſion in public affairs was made; and, leaſt magiſtrates ſhould err in their duty, they are injoined to have a copy of the law for their private peruſal, and to devote a part of every day to the ſtudy of it. " * When thou art come unto the land, which the Lord thy God giveth thee, and ſhalt poſſeſs it, and ſhalt dwell therein, and ſhalt ſay, I will ſet a king over me, like as all the nations which are about me : Thou ſhalt, in any wiſe, ſet him king over thee, whom the Lord thy God ſhall chuſe. And it ſhall be, when he ſitteth upon the throne of his kingdom, that he ſhall write him a copy of this law in a book, out of that which is before the Prieſts the Levites : And it ſhall be with him, and he ſhall read therein all the days of his life ; that he may learn to fear the Lord his God, to keep all the words of this law, and theſe ſtatutes to do them."

The ſame principle is laid down for the direction of ſubordinate rulers, with this additional circumſtance, " † that in matters of difficulty, they ſhould have recourſe to the Prieſts, whoſe office it was to expound the law, and that the ſentence pronounced by them ſhould be final."

The conduct of Iſrael, for many ages, was generally conformable with this precept ; and on great political emergencies, the circumſtances of which came not immediately under the notice of the law, the Prieſts or the Prophets were conſulted, and their voices implicitly obeyed.

If the politics of the Jews were thus ſubjected to the morality of their religion ; does it not evidently follow that the ſame morality, under the goſpel of diſpenſation, ſhould regulate, with commanding influence, the politics of ſtates profeſſing chriſtianity ? This concluſion is ſo juſt and obvious, that it cannot be denied ; and I am convinced it will be adopted in this aſſembly, with that candor and cordiality, which its importance juſtly claims.

In the ſtrength of this conviction, permit me to ſubjoin a few plain inferences from what hath been diſcourſed on this ſubject. And 1ſt. As the kingdom of Chriſt is not of this world—As it did not originate from worldly policy ; doth not join iſſue with the

C

* Deut. 17, 14, 15, 18, 19. † Deut. 17, 8, 13.

passions or prejudices of men; disclaims the aid of violence and oppression; and arrogates to itself no authority but what truth and righteousness should possess over the minds and conduct of men: we may infer that every attempt to influence belief, or regulate modes of worship among men, by human policy or power, is inconsistent with its spirit. It is a kingdom purely moral and religious; morality and religion are personal; and the religious belief of every individual must depend upon the light in which religious subjects are presented to his understanding.

2dly. As christianity proposes the happiness of mankind as its end, prohibits the violation of his person, character, and property, and denounces its judgements against those who counteract it; we may infer that every act of perfidy, oppression, cruelty, and injustice is highly offensive to that merciful and righteous God, from whom it derives its solemn sanction. If this inference be just, in respect to individuals who fill private walks of life; it cannot be less so, in regard to those, who, from more elevated stations extend their influence through a wider circle; or states, the effects of whose rapacity and ambition, are still more dreadfully destructive. As Jesus came to subdue the passions of men, direct them into proper channels, and regulate their influence; all offensive wars, for wealth, empire, fame, or even religion itself, are evidently inconsistent with his character and dominion. We can never suppose that he would forbid the poor man to purloin a morsel of bread, or lift his hand against his neighbour, under pain of damnation, and yet, suffer the great to plunder and destroy with impunity; or states to deluge the earth with blood. The thought is too big with absurdity to find reception, for a moment, into an enlightened mind.

To us, my Revd. Fathers and brethren, who hold the character of Ministers, under the Messiah's kingdom, what hath been offered upon this subject, applies with more than common force. We have undertaken the dispensation of a trust, the most important which can be committed to mortals—A trust, on the discharge of which, it is universally acknowledged, the improvement and virtue of multitudes depend. Nor do the duties of our office affect men as individuals only. From the connexion of religion with politics, and the authority which she claims over the kingdoms of the world, we derive a political character highly important, and become the dispensers of that knowledge, which unfolds and ought to regulate their political interefts; and patrons of that virtue which alone can fecure them. While, therefore, we point the way to Heaven in our religious character, let us not forget the duties of the other; or the additional weight which love of country may give to the diftant profpects of futurity. Let us confider that while true patriotifm ftands on virtue as its bafe, it rears its head above the regions of mortality, and claims an intereft in that eternal world where truth and righteoufnefs fhall reign for ever, without controul: And let us endeavour to infufe into the minds of our people a full perfuafion that ftrict honor, incorruptible integrity, and inviolable attachment to truth and righteoufnefs, are abfolutely neceffary to national profperity; and that without them patriotifm is a bubble, and religion only an empty name.

The prefent fituation of this our native country, affords us but too many melancholy opportunities of introducing and inculcating this interefting truth. While every village murmurs complaints againft the corruption of fuperiors, and charges the reprefentatives of the people, and the nobility of the nation, with corruption, venality, and evil defign, are not we called upon to remind them that their own meannefs, venality, and corruption are the fources of all? Do not the reprefentatives derive their powers from the voice of the people? And doth not the people—that very people which complains fo loudly—proftitute its voice for a fmile—a promife— nay, a nights debauch? If our duty binds us to reprove and exhort, furely here reproof and exhortation are loudly called for; and by adminiftering them, in due feafon, we would check corruption at its fources, and become the guardians of that liberty which is the parent of national profperity, and fource of every earthly bleffing.

Further, we ought particularly to cherifh and diffue that liberal fpirit in religion, which views the Redeemer as fole Lord in his own kingdom; and all chriftians as *his* fubjects, and accountable *to him alone in religious matters.* We fhould endeavour to banifh that blind and tyrannic dæmon which can fee no worth, but in the name of party, and under the claim of liberty, is bufied only in the forgery of chains. We have much reafon to rejoice and be thankful, that the influence of this dæmon hath long been declining in our country. That it may foon be annihilated for ever is an event devoutly to be wifhed! We have lately feen toleration extend her foothing arms, and offer an embrace unknown before.

Let us rejoice in the prospect which this opens before us; and let us join our helping hand to extend them wider still. Since policy hath so far foregone her claims over religion, let us endeavour to raise the kingdom of Christ to its proper dignity, and reduce its connexion with the kingdoms of the world, to those principles by which we ought to be regulated for ever.

SERMON II.

LUKE 2. 14. *"Glory to God in the higheft, and on earth Peace—Good-will towards Men."*

THE appearance of Chrift is truly worthy of attention, admiration, and joy, in all its circumftances. The early period at at which it was foretold, the varity and precifion of the prophecies concerning it, the earneftnefs with which it was expected, the nature and extent of the bleffings which it was to diffufe, and the aftonifhing manner in which it was announced, are equally remarkable.

The earneftnefs with which he was expected, may be eafily accounted for, from the glories in which prophecy had delineated his kingdom, as to extent, duration, and fupremacy ; the revolutions it would occafion, and the bleffings it would difpenfe. And the univerfality, of this expectation arofe from the fucceffive difperfions of the Jewifh people among the nations of the earth. In each of thefe they diffufed a knowledge of their religion, their prophecies, and the events to which they pointed. And this knowledge, though greatly adulterated, in the impure channels through which it flowed, was preferved by tradition, till the coming of the fon of man—the feed promifed to Abraham, in which " all the nations of the earth fhould be bleffed."—Its traces are faid to be very difcernible in the remaining fragments of eaftern antiquity; they abound in the earlieft monuments of Grecian literature; and from the fame fource, fome of the fineft pictures in Roman poetry, feem to have borrowed their brighteft colouring.

The character in which Chrift was expected, equally commands veneration and love. As a conqueror fubduing nations, bringing thrones, dominions, and principalities under fubjection, and eftablifhing an univerfal empire, he appears with unequalled grandeur. But when we confider him as founding this empire on the eternal principles of juftice, extending it by truth, fupporting it by righteoufnefs, cementing it by univerfal love, and good-will among men, and blending with its very effence, the feeds and the bleffings of peace; he appears in all the charms of native lovelinefs— the image of divinity, and glory of man!

In this laft character, he is commonly exhibited by the prophets; and his kingdom delineated as a kingdom of peace. And in allufion to it, his birth is announced by Angels, as " tidings of great joy," with circumftances becoming the greatnefs of the event.—Circumftances, compared with which, the birth-night pageantry of earthly princes, with all the blaze of illumination, the pompous ode of a laurelled hireling, and the fafhionable congratulations of the gayeft court, appear as the mimickry of fantaftic children. An angel of God is the herald, who proclaims the nativity of Sion's King—not to a crowded levee of expecting fycophants in a fplendid palace—but to a few fimple fhepherds, in the fields of Bethlehem! Indication fure, that with innocence alone peace can dwell. A light fupernatural—Emblem expreffive of the glory of the Lord—illuminates the fcene; while Seraphs chant the enraptured fong: " Glory to God in the higheft; and on earth peace—Good-will towards men!"

What were the feelings of the fimple fhepherds during this fcene of fplendour and magnificence? Fear, curiofity, aftonifhment, and joy, muft have occupied their fouls in quick fucceffion;

We are told indeed, that fear alone poffeffed them, on the firft appearance of the Angel, and the unaccountable brightnefs, with which they were furrounded. " They were fore afraid." But we may naturally fuppofe that this was immediately difpelled, when the angel thus addreffed them, with foothing words." Fear not ! for behold, I bring you good tidings of great joy, which fhall be unto *all people.*"

As thefe words would naturally difpel their fears, they would as naturally excite their curiofity to know the tidings, fraught with good, not to a family or nation, but to *all people.* And when they were told that it was the birth of a Saviour—a long and anxiouf-ly expected Saviour—" Who was Chrift, the Lord ;" and heard it celebrated with Seraph's fong ; aftonifhment and joy muft have filled their hearts.

Though thefe circumftances muft have made the firft and ftrong-eft impreffions on the minds of the fhepherds ; yet, when the an-gels departed, and the fupernatural light difappeared, they recol-lected one lefs ftricking, but of great importance, concerning which they wifely determined to be fatisfied. When the Angel annonnced the birth of a Saviour, he told them that it had taken place in the city of David : And, as even this was not fufficiently explicit, he added, for their fatisfaction : " This fhall be a fign unto you ;" viz. that all I have told you is true—" Ye fhall find the babe, wrapped in fwaddling clothes, lying in a manger."

Had not fome fuch circumftance been propofed for their future in-veftigation, they might probably have concluded, from the tumultu-ous emotions excited by the wondrous fcene, and the aftonifhment in which it left them, that it might be only a fplendid illufion, paffing before the fancy in a dream or trance. But if the under-ftanding could be fatisfied, that it was real, there was no room for doubt concerning the reft. They, therefore, refolved to go im-mediately to Bethlehem ; and as it appears, to fay nothing of what they had feen and heard, till they knew whether a new-born child, fo circumftanced, could be found there. " When the Angels were gone, they faid, one to another, let us now go, even unto Bethlehem, and fee this thing which hath come to pafs, which the Lord hath made known to us. And they came with hafte, and found Mary and Jofeph, and the babe lying in a manger. And when they had seen it, they made known *publicly*, the saying which was told them concerning this child."

The prudent caution of the shepherds on this occasion, is not more honorable to them, than instructive to the world. Nor is it to be doubted but the Evangelist had a view to such instruction, in the minute detail he has given of their conduct. And had it been attended to, ten thousand dreams of wild imagination, which superstition or enthusiasm has fondly laid hold of, and published to the world, as revelations from God, would have been buried in silence, or rejected with contempt.

Be this as it may, the calm and prudent circumspection of the shepherds, in examining the circumstances of this astonishing scene, as it reflects honor on their memories, so it has secured credit to their narrative through all succeeding generations. Convinced as we are of its truth, nothing remains for us, as matter of inquiry, but the meaning of the Angel's song; "glory to God in the highest; and on earth peace—good-will towards men;" and the improvement which we ought to make of it; as the professed subjects of "Christ the Lord."

And surely, no inquiry could come before us, with more propriety, on the day which we commemorate as the anniversary of his birth—A day, which, while many of our profession are profaning by riot and debauchery, I trust we are devoting to better purposes.

But while I say this, I would not be thought to give the particular observance of this day a place in the catalogue of prescribed duties. Such observance is no where enjoined by Christ himself; nor has it any sanction, that I can find, either from the writings or example of his Apostles. Still, however, I am convinced, as the observance is kept up, it is better to apply it to religious services, than spend it in dissipation, drunkenness, and blasphemy—a practice equally injurious to religion, inconsistent with the purpose of a Saviour's coming, and dishonorable to men.

In this conviction, let us proceed to the inquiries already mentioned, as arising from the Angel's song.

In Scripture, the phrases " to praise," and " give glory," are every where ufed in the fame fenfe. And that this is a fong of praife, is evident, from the manner in which it is introduced "There was, with the Angel, a multitude of the heavenly hoft praifing God," and faying, "Glory to God:" that is, "praife be to God," or, "let God be praifed."

Commentators have widely, though as it appears, unneceffarily differed about the meaning of the words, "in the higheft." Some refer them to the degree of praife, fome to the rank of the beings offered it, and others to the place in which it is offered. According to the firft, it fignifies, , "let God be praifed in the higheft degree;" the fecond, "by the higheft orders of Angels;" and the third, "in the higheft Heavens."

I fay, this difference feems trifling and unneceffary, as all the three circumftances, to which they point, are nearly, if not infeparably connected. According to common conception, the higheft Heavens are the habitation of the moft exalted Angels; and from the fuperior clearnefs of their perceptions of divine excellence, and the fublimity of their fentiments, their praifes muft be expreffed in the loftieft ftrains which fpirit can conceive, or language utter.

However, if thefe circumftances are to be feparated, I am convinced the phrafe principally relates to the higheft orders of created beings, or Angels. In this I am confirmed by the manner in which it is expreffed in the original, as connected with the laft phrafe in the verfe, which undoubtedly ought to be rendered, "good-will among men." The fong would then ftand thus: "Glory to God among the higheft: and on earth peace—Goodwill among men." And the meaning is plainly this; that in the birth of Meffiah, foundation is laid for everlafting praife among the heavenly hofts, and peace and goodwill among men on earth.

That the appearance of Meffiah was an event, which had engaged the attention, and given fcope to the miniftration of Angels, from the earlieft ages of the world, we cannot doubt, as many of the promifes and prophecies concerning it, were delivered through them. That they did not fully comprehend the great fcheme to be executed by him; or the manner in, and means by which it was to be accomplifhed, till they faw them in the event, we have ftrong reafons to believe. To this we are led by

D

the declaration of the Apoſtle Peter: " Into which things the Angels deſire to look ;" that is, the things which the Prophets had foretold, and the accompliſhment of which the preachers of the goſpel then reported to the perſons, to whom the Apoſtle wrote.

On the ſuppoſition of this their ignorance, and on it alone, their curioſity, or deſire to look into the things concerning Chriſt, can be accounted for: And by this curioſity, they would be incited to trace the hand of God, through all his diſpenſations to the poſterity of Abraham, till the promiſed ſeed appeared.

In this purſuit, the varieties of fortune, which they experienced, their diviſions among themſelves, their diſperſions and captivities, which frequently threatened their extinction as a nation, and ſpread a ſhade of improbability over the face of prophecy, would all appear before them. And the removal of this, by the full accompliſhment of what was foretold, would enliven their ſentiments of wonder, devotion, and joy, and give new animation to their ſongs of praiſe. To ſee all the various links of prophecy, continued in one uninterrupted chain, through 1600 years, terminating in the event of a moment— to ſee all improbalities ſwallowed up in certainty—and the hidden things of ages irradiated by a luſtre, bright as the glory of the Lord, muſt have raiſed admiration to the higheſt, and dictated a praiſe equally ſublime !

Nor would the directing hand of ſovereign wiſdom, in conducting circumſtances to the accompliſhment of this momentous event, diſplay more clearly the ſteadfaſtneſs of the counſels of God, than the happy revolution to which it was preparatory, would exhibit the riches of his grace—grace to a world, long involved in wretchedneſs, through the blindneſs and corruption of their own hearts, and their unnatural barbarities, one to another.

From a circumſtance already mentioned, in the character and office of Angels, we cannot ſuppoſe them ignorant, either of the character or condition of men. By them, as was obſerved, many intimations of the will of God were communicated. With accounts of theſe, the Old Teſtament abounds, from beginng to end. Hence they are characterized as " miniſtering ſpirits, who miniſter to thoſe ſhall be heirs of ſalvation." In theſe miniſtrations, they muſt have become acquainted with the miſeries of man, and all the sources from which they spring. And as Job introduces them as witnesses of the first creation, and " shouting for joy," when the morning stars, in harmonious order, proclaimed their Maker's praise---As they were no strangers to him, in his native state of innocence and peace---and now witnessed the appearance of Messiah, king of righteousness, and promised prince of peace and love ; man must be an object familiar to them, in all the variety of dignity and meanness, innocence and guilt, happiness and misery, through which he has passed.

Nor are we left to suppose that their feelings for him are less sensible, than their knowledge of him is clear. Love is the character, the life, and the spirit of Heaven. And where love is, misery must call forth the sensation of sorrow ; and the prospect, or contemplation of happiness excite joy. Accordingly, our Saviour informs us, " that there is joy in the presence of Angels, on the repentance of a sinner." There must, therefore, be sorrow on the apostacy of a Saint. And if the conduct and fate of an individual can excite even the weakest emotion in heavenly minds, the wickedness or recovery---the misery or happiness of a world, must be an object infinitely more affecting.

If this idea be just, as it appears rational, what must have been the feelings of Angels, for the degeneracy and wretchedness of man, fallen from his native dignity, and lost to innocence ! They had seen him rise from his maker's hand, with form erect, countenance elevated towards Heaven, and the image of divinity imprinted on his soul ! They had seen him enrobed in native innocence, and rejoicing in conscious integrity ! They had seen him, also, become vain in his imagination, entangled in the multitude of his own inventions, enslaved by corruption, and groaning under the chains of guilt and wretchedness : They had seen him at enmity with God---at enmity with himself---without peace---without hope---and without a comforter !

In exact proportion to the compassion and sorrow which these gloomy scenes called forth, must have been the joy of Angels on the appearance of a Saviour fraught with the tidings of salvation, the blessings of peace, and the seeds of benevolence and goodwill among men. And as this Saviour was the messenger of Heaven ---the spontaneous gift of the father's love---for the redemption, recovery, and reconciliation of an enslaved and distracted world, generofity and devotion muſt have jointly inſpired the angelic ſong of gratulation and praiſe. " Glory to God among the higheſt ; on earth peace ; goodwill among men !

What was thus a ſubject of praiſe and congratulation to Angels, who were only the meſſengers of glad tidings to others, ſhould ſurely be a ſubject of gratitude and joy to men—men, to whom this peace was proclaimed, and among whom, goodwill, as its parent, was to be cheriſhed for ever.

That we may ſee this with clearneſs, and learn the improvement to which it leads, let us now conſider the extent and importance of the peace here proclaimed.

Peace with God is the foundation of human hope, and human happineſs. This peace is repreſented in ſcripture, as violated by idolatry, and every kind of wickedneſs. The former is called enmity againſt God, as depoſing him from his ſovereignty, and placing an idol in his ſtead ; the latter, as violating his authority, and withholding that allegiance which is due to him, as Lord of the univerſe. Peace with him, therefore, is reſtored in the one caſe, by reclaiming men from idolatry, to the belief, acknowledgment, and worſhip of him alone, as " the only living and true God ;" and in the other, by turning them from their iniquities into the paths of righteouſneſs. As theſe effects were eminently produced by the revelation of Chriſt, and of him alone, he is emphatically called " our peace :" And the Apoſtle declares, that " we have peace with God, through our Lord Jeſus Chriſt."

In this particular, the extent and importance of the peace proclaimed by the Angels, is obvious and amazing. It reaches wide as the belief of the goſpel has been, now is, or ever will be. It is important, as the firſt principle of true religion, with all the bleſſings of which it is productive. And how great that importance is, we may eaſily judge, by comparing the ſtate even of the moſt ignorant nations of the chriſtian world with thoſe who ſit in darkneſs—" who know not God, and obey not the Goſpel." But what ſhall be its importance, when its extent ſhall become wide as the habitable world ! When the fullneſs of the heathen ſhall become the inheritance of Chriſt, and the uttermoſt parts of the earth his poſſeſſion ! When enmity ſhall ceaſe, and the univerſal prevalence of the Gospel shall unite the hearts of men in peace with God !

This leads us to a second circumstance implied in the peace here announced ; that is, peace among men, in the exercise. of that worship, of which God is the only proper object. In the heathen world, nation had been separated from nation, through all ages, by the diversity and opposition of their religious rites, and the objects of their devotion. Hence in their contests, not only men were considered as at war with men, but gods with gods. Between all of them and the Jews, this diversity was the source of mutual contempt and enmity, from an abuse of the precepts, by which the seed of Abraham were enjoined to avoid intercourse with them, " lest they should be corrupted by their example." Every heathen was prohibited from their society, till he became a convert to their religion ; and even then, he was not admitted to a fulness of communion. He could neither hold an office in their temple, nor be admitted into its inner court. Circumcision, the seal of the Abrahamic covenant, was a never failing source of enmity and reproach. Without submission to it, no heathen could be admitted into religious communion.

This mark of distinction, though necessary for a time, yet inviduous from its abuse, was abolished by Christ ; and Jew and Gentile united by his Gospel, in community of religious rights, equality of privilege, and the bonds of peace. The view of this reconciliation given by the Apostle Paul, in opposition to the Judaizing teachers, who argued for the continuance of Mosaical distinctions, is equally just and elegant. The quotation is long, but should not be overlooked. " Remember," saith he to the converts from the Heathen at Ephesus—" Remember that *ye,* formerly Gentiles in the flesh, called uncircumcision, by that which is called circumcision in the flesh, made by hands, were at that time without Christ, being aliens from the commonwealth of Israel, and strangers to the covenant of promise ; having no hope, and without God in the world : But now in Christ Jesus, ye who were formerly far off, have been made nigh, by the blood of Christ. For he is *our peace,* who hath made both *one,* and hath broken down the middle wall of partition between us, having abolished in his flesh, the *enmity, the law of commandments, in ordinances,* to make in himself of *twain, one* new man—making peace ; and that he might reconcile *both* unto God, in *one* body, by the cross, having slain the *enmity* thereby; and came and preached *peace* to you, who were afar off, and to them who were nigh. For through him, we have both access to the Father by one spirit. Now, therefore, ye are no more strangers and foreigners, but fellow-citizens with the Saints, and of the household of God."

Important as these two particulars are, there is a third of equal, if not superior importance, implied in " the peace" which was sung by Angels, in the fields of Bethlehem—I say, *superior importance ;* as without *it,* neither peace with God, nor harmony in his worshship, can be enjoyed or subsist. That is, peace among the individuals, neighbourhoods, and nations of men, founded on mutual and universal goodwill.

God is the common father of the universe : the nations of men are his family on earth ; and consequently, connected by the relation of brethren. To him, therefore, they can never unite in the devotion of children, while their hearts are alienated from each other by envy, enmity, and strife. Nay, while they are strangers to that mutual goodwill, which is the parent of peace among men, they must be incapable of that love of God, which is essential to his worship. This seems to be the meaning of the Apostle John : " If any man say, I love God, and hate his brother, he is a liar ; for he who loveth not his brother, whom he hath seen, how can he love God, whom he hath not seen ! He who loveth not, knoweth not God ; but he who dwelleth in love, dwelleth in God, and God in him." On this principle, that love and peace among men are essential to peace and acceptance with God, our Saviour appears to have founded the following precept. " If thou bring thy gift to the altar, and there rememberest that thy brother hath aught aginst thee ; leave there thy gift before the altar, and go thy way : first be reconciled to thy brother, and then come and offer thy gift." Thus it is, that as the seeds of peace are sown in the doctrines of Jesus, the services of his religion are its restoratives and guardians among men.

That this peace is one great object of Messiah's appearance is further evident, not only from the warmth with which that love is inculcated, from which it springs ; and the declarations, that " love is the end of the commandment," and " fulfilling of the law ;" but from the practice and instructions of Christ himself, and the inſtructions of his Apoſtles to all the churches. " Peace be to this houſe," was the introductory ſalutation, with which he ſent his Diſciples to all the families of Iſrael. " Have peace one with another," was his inſtruction to themſelves; and " Peace be unto you," the words in which he addreſſed them after his re-reſurrection. The declarations of the Apoſtle are: " God hath called us to peace. The fruit of the Spirit is love and peace: and the kingdom of God is not meat and drink; but righteouſ-neſs, and peace, and joy in the Holy Spirit." Hence ariſe the precepts which they inculcate: " Let the peace of God rule in your hearts: Keep the unity of the Spirit in the bonds of peace: Seek peace, and enſure it; and as much as in you lieth, live peaceably with all men."

Theſe, and a thouſand other paſſages, clearly ſhew, that the ſpirit of chriſtianity is a ſpirit of peace. And the laſt plainly de-monſtrates, that " the way of peace," into which its author came to lead us, extends to " the ends of the earth," and that the goodwill from which it ſprings, embraces the whole family of men: that it ſhould not be limited by country, climate, or com-plexion—by modes of religion, or forms of government: and that the political fiction of a natural enmity between any nations or ſocieties of men, is blaſphemy againſt nature, and nature's God. This is admirably illuſtrated by the example of the bene-volent Jeſus. The compaſſion of his heart, and the bounty of his healing hand, were as ready for a Samaritan, who worſhipped the calves of Jeroboam, or a Roman centurion who adored the dæmons of the nations, as the poor and afflicted of the houſe of Iſrael. And in his commiſſion to the Apoſtles, he ſent to all, with the tidings of ſalvaation, the doctrine of peace.

Nor are we left to ſuppoſe, that the bleſſings of peace, and obligations to purſue it, are confined to men as individuals. Na-tions are repreſented in the glowing language of prophecy, as ob-jects of Meſſiah's peace, and actuated by its ſpirit. Thus ſaith Iſaiah: " He ſhall judge among the nations, and rebuke many people: and they ſhall beat their ſwords into plough-ſhares, and their ſpears into pruning-hooks: Nation ſhall not lift up ſword a-gainſt nation; neither ſhall they learn war any more."

The effects of this happy revolution, when wars ſhall ceaſe, and the ſword of violence be ſheathed for ever—When the ſavage tyrant shall lay aside his ferocity, the timid slave be raised to the dignity and privileges of man, and the sweets of social intercourse enjoyed by all, in security and repose, are elegantly painted in another passage, by the hand of the same master. " The wolf shall dwell with the lamb, and the leopard shall lie down with the kid, and the calf and the young lion, and the fatling together ; and a little child shall lead them. And the cow and the bear shall feed ; their young ones shall lie down together ; and the lion shall eat straw like the ox. And the sucking child shall play on the hole of the asp, and the weaned child shall put his hand on the adder's den. They shall not hurt nor destroy in all my holy mountain : for the earth shall be full of the knowledge of the Lord, as the waters cover the sea."

What a delightful scene is here exhibited, in the glowing language of prophetic ardor, as characterizing Messiah's reign ! A scene, where under the bold and expressive figures of the ravening wolf dwelling with the lamb, around whose fold he had prowled for prey ; and the *panther, ferocious tyrant of the mountain,* lying down with the kid—the lion, *savage monarch of the hill,* eating straw with the ox, and herding with the calf and the fatling—and the *bear of the rock, forgetting his ferocity and growling,* feeding with the cow—we are taught to look forward to a period, when rapine shall cease, oppression be no more, violence unheard of, and confidence, harmony, and peace, established among the nations—And when the hand of the assassin, and the envenomed tongue of the secret slanderer, aptly represented by the adder lurking in his den, shall not dare to wound even the suckling child !

Thus have I endeavoured to point out the extent and importance of the peace on earth, of which Messiah was the messenger and the fountain. I have shewn, from the indisputable testimony of the Bible, that it implies reconciliation to God, as the only object of religious worship ; union among men, in the enjoyment of religious rights, equality of religious privilege, and the bonds of love ; and the establishment of goodwill, harmony, and peace among all the individuals, families, neighbourhoods, and nations of the world we inhabit.

From these circumstances, taken together, I trust it is evident, that the prospect opened by the birth of Messiah, was sufficient to infpire Angels with admiration and joy, warm the hearts of men with gratitude, and unite them by goodwill.

But while we rejoice in the profpect, and admit the folidity of the principles, on which Angels fung ; we muft feel aftonifhment and regret, that a profpect fo pleafing has never been fully realized.

It is true, for upwards of three hundred years after the publication of the gofpel, the mutual affection of chriftians, and the peaceablenefs of their demeanour, were fubjects of wonder, even to their enemies. But no fooner was their religion connected with the politics of the kingdoms, and the intrigues of ftatefmen, and their priefts feated among *nobles,* and ranked with the princes of the earth, than the bond of union was broken, the mild fpirit of religion fwallowed up by ambition, and the light of the gofpel converted into a firebrand of difcord. That the paffions of individuals had introduced perfonal difputes, before this period, the Apoftles inform us ; but that thefe ever affected the public harmony, we have no reafon to believe. However, from the days of Conftantine, in which the honors and emoluments of the ftate were connected with party or office in the religion of Jefus, down to the prefent, peace has been interrupted in the chriftian world ; and the luft of power, riches, and pleafure has been ftronger, not only than the obligations of religion, but the ties of nature. Of this, the hiftory of fourteen hundred years is a continued teftimony ; and the prefent moment is an unhappy demonftration. In all the religious contefts which have diftracted nations, and terminated fo often in fcenes of blood, *the religion of the ftate,* and not the religion of Jefus, has been the fubject, and the love of power, pre-eminence, or riches, the leading principle. And whatever party prevailed, fufficient care was taken to humble the vanquifhed, fink them into infignificance, and brand them with infamy. Nor can we attribute this fpirit *exclufively,* to any church, fect, or party. It has uniformly diffufed itfelf *through* all, and operated *in* all. Of this, the lands of our nativity have afforded melancholy, but undenible examples. During the reigns of the Stuart family, all parties were favoured in turn ; and as power changed fides, Catholic burned Proteftant, Proteftant perfecuted Catholic, and the Prefbyterians in their momentary triumph, denied toleration to both. In later periods, we fee the fame fcenes acted in all their parts. We fee Scottifh Prefbyterians profcribe epifcopacy ;

E

English episcopalians exclude Presbyterians from the honors and offices of the state; and a Scion of the same stock, transplanted to Ireland, shedding its baneful influence over the Presbyterians, who first gave that stability to its root, which has clothed its branches with fruits of gold. And over all, we see the devoted Catholics bound down with the twisted chains of mental darkness, and corporal incapacity, by a body of laws, which humanity views with horror, justice reprobates, and religion pronounces *accursed.*

Blessed Jesus! are these the fruits of that peace on earth—that goodwill among men—the seeds of which thou camest to sow? *No!!!* They have sprung up in thy field, from the tares which the enemy sowed, in the night of darkness, while men slept. Thanks be to God! that darkness is no more; and men have awaked from the sleep of torpid indolence. The dawn of knowledge opens upon their understanding, and their hearts are warmed by its enlivening rays. The poisonous plants are already known by their fruits, and ere the day reaches its meridian brightness, they shall be plucked up by the roots, bound up in bundles, and cast into the fire. Then, and not till then, will the prophecies of God, and the prospects of Angels, be realized among us—Then will jealousies cease, discontents vanish, animosities be extinguished, and the pure spirit of the gospel, unadulterated by the politics of the world, warm us into mutual kindness, restore us to confidence, and soothe us into peace.

The same causes, which have rendered the *peace of the gospel* an empty name and banished it from among christians, have hitherto prevented the *extension of the gospel* to the other nations of the world. The covetousness, rapacity, cruelty, and violence of the professors of christianity, have universally caused the name of God to be blasphemed among the heathen, and the religion of Messiah to be rejected. Of this we have many instances in the conquest of America by the Spaniards; and it is not improbable, that succeeding generations will be informed of the like barbarities, practised by our own countrymen, in the east; though few of them have been yet published among us. These enormities, while they strike us with horror, and cover humanity with a blush, enable us to assign a reason, why the knowledge of the Lord hath not yet overflowed the earth, as the waters cover the sea: and at the same time convince us, that the peace of the gospel can never prevail among men, till the passions, the political interests, and the domineering fpirit of religious party, be fwallowed up in the ocean of univerfal goodwill.

If profpects may be trufted, that blifsful period is at hand, even at the door. One great and enlightened nation has burft the chains of prejudice and flavery, difclaimed the idea of conqueft for dominion, opened the temple of liberty for all religious denominations at home, and fent forth her arms, *not to deftroy*, but *reftore* the liberty of the world, and extend her bleffings to all who dare, and by daring, deferve to be free. Tyrants already tremble at her name; while oppreffed nations exult in her fuccefs, receive her fons with gratitude and joy, and unite in her caufe. Happy! thrice happy the people, whofe rulers may become wife, by the leffon which fhe has been obliged to write in letters of blood— Where the ear of the Prince may be open to the voice of humanity reciting her grievances, and fupplicating redrefs; and the neceffity and horrors of revolution precluded, by *feafonable* and *radical* reform! That this may be our cafe is the prayer of my heart. That national "juftice may roll down as waters, and righteoufnefs as a mighty ftream"—that civil pains and penalties, on account of religion, may be abolifhed for ever—and that *equal liberty—equal privilege*, and *equal protection*, may henceforth, be the portion of *all* the people; unite them in the bonds of inviolable brotherhood; and *perpetuate their attachment to their king and conftitution*, by a community of intereft in the peace and profperity of their country!

From the views which have been given, of the peace to be introduced by the gofpel, and the caufes which have hitherto prevented its eftablifhment and extenfion, the improvement to which it leads is plain and obvious.

That peace on earth; that is, among all the members of the great family of men, who inhabit it, is an end of the gofpel, we have clearly feen. And that it affords the means, and enforces the duty of obtaining and preferving it, in the principles which it prefcribes, and the motives it supplies, we cannot deny. We have feen alfo, that this peace has been prevented or deftroyed, by the inordinate paffions, and unjuftifiable practices, both of individuals and nations, through every age, and in every country. With regard to the whole, the inquiry of the Apoftle James, and the anfwer which accompanies it, may be juftly applied: " Whence come wars and fightings among you ? Come they not hence, even of your lufts. Ye luft, and have not ; ye kill and defire to have ; ye fight and war, yet ye cannot obtain."

If this be founded in truth, and fupported by experience ; and if the peace of the gofpel be an object of defire, thefe lufts fhould be reftrained, in order to attain it. If the covetoufnefs, ambition, cruelty, and haughtinefs of men, have been the parents of ftrife, oppreffion, bloodfhed, confufion, and every evil work, in families, neighbourhoods, and nations, let thefe be rooted out, and mode-ration, juftice, and humility, planted in their ftead, and peace, with all her bleffings, will immediately follow. The native off-fpring of the gofpel are, patience, forbearance, gentlenefs, goodnefs, and temperance, and her genuine fruits, peace and joy.

Hence, then, an obvious improvement of the fubject before us. As chriftians, as men, and members of a ftate, we fhould mortify and fubdue our felfifh, turbulent, and ambitious paffions —We fhould reftrain the malevolence of our tongues, and with-draw our hands from fecret fraud and open violence—we fhould retract every falfhood we have uttered, make reparation for the injuries we have done, and candidly acknowledge the offences we have committed againft our brethren, that they may return to us, in the fpirit of forgiving meeknefs, and reftore us to their confi-dence, efteem, and love. In like manner, in whatever we have been injured or offended, fo foon as our offending brother fhall make reafonable reparation for the evil he hath done us, or becom-ing acknowledgement of his offence, we fhould cordially receive him with the arms of forgivenefs—We fhould immediately " put away all bitternefs and wrath, and anger, and clamour, and evil-fpeaking, with all malice ; and be kind one to another, tender-hearted, forgiving one another, even as God, for Chrift's fake, hath forgiven us."

A fecond improvement of this fubject, of no fmall importance, arifes from a melancholy circumftance, which the wife and good have long obferved, and deeply regretted : that is, violations of friendfhip, and difturbance of peace between individuals, families, and neighbourhoods, without injury or offence, actual or intend-ed, on the part of either. This arifes from attention to an order of beings, in the form of men, called in Scripture, " bufy-bodies, tattlers, or tale-bearers. They are to the mind of man, nearly the same as vermin to the bodies of brutes, which, at first *tickle,* but in the end, *teaze* and *torment.*" It has been observed also, that the greater animals are chiefly infested by vermin ; and that the leanest and feeblest have the greater number. The same is observable among men. The great are perpetually haunted by tale-bearers ; and if one can be found of a feeble understanding, and meagree brain, they cluster round him, and tickle his ears with enconiums on his own importance, till they gain admittance. Hence, they may be justly compared to a noxious insect, which is said to enter the ear of the rein-deer, eat its way into the brain, and produce madness. These tattlers are generally animals of little judgment, and less goodness ; but of considerable cunning, and unbounded malice. They can pervert what they hear, misrepresent what they see, and call up a creation of falshood, on occasion, to serve a turn. So early as the days of Moses, their character seems to have been well known, and their occupation so odious, that it was strictly forbidden to the people of Israel. " Thou shalt not go up and down as a tale-bearer ; neither shalt thou stand against the blood of thy neighbour." They appear, likewise to have crept in, very early, among the first christians. The Apostle Paul describes them as worthless vagabonds, " idle, wandering about from house to house, and speaking things they ought not." And Peter classes them with " thieves and murderers." Even now, we have reason to believe, that some such there are. The jealousies, strifes, and enmities, which so frequently separate friend from friend, neighbour from neighbour, and family from family ; and inflame larger societies with mutual jealousies, apprehension, and animosities, clearly prove it ; if we can believe the testimony of the wise Solomon. " Where no wood is, there the fire goeth out, so, where there is no tale-bearer, strife ceaseth. But as coals are to burning coals, and wood to wood ; so is a malicious man to kindle discord. The words of a tale-bearer are as wounds ; they go down into the chambers of the belly. For a froward man soweth strife, and a whisperer separateth chief friends."

From this circumstance the improvement is obvious. If we value the peace, we have been considering as we ought ; and from a sense of its importance, wish to preserve it—If, for this purpose, we are willing to acknowledge the offences we have committed, and repair the injuries we have done ; and in order to secure it, keep a watch upon our hands, our hearts, and our tongues, in all time to come; should we not, likewise, shut our ears against the poison of the slanderer, the malicious whisperer's artful tale, the base insinuations of the cringing sycophant, and the false representations of the officious partizan? Reason says, " it is right" —Prudence says, " it is our interest"—Religion says, " it is our duty"—and experience proclaims, with ten thousand tongues, that " if we do not, jealousies, discord, and strife will reign for ever— that Heaven-born peace will be eternally banished from the society, and soothing comfort from the hearts of men."

Let us then, be determined to obey their united voice. Let us no longer listen to the tale of malice, or of art, which tends to deceive, to irritate and inflame; and by representing men as enemies to each other, to convert them into such. And if this be our duty, where the misrepresentation extends, only to an individual, or a family; it is, if possible, *more than duty*, where it goes to calumniate and vilify, not only a neighbourhood, but a nation; by calumny and falshood, to revive and inflame mutual prejudice, jealousy, and contention; and under their influence, to perpetuate oppression, slavery, and wretchedness.

Such are the slanders, now and lately inculcated among you, against which your ears should be shut, and your hearts double-fortified. The subject of these are the Roman Catholics of Ireland—*three fourths of its inhabitants*. Ye are told by malicious and designing men, that they are not only " *ignorant*, but *incapable of liberty*."

The latter part of this assertion, is a *libel* on *human nature*, and *blasphemy against God!* The wretch must be equally lost to religion and shame, who dares assert that God is so weak, or so wicked, as to form a nation of men, insensible to the first right of humanity, and incapable of enjoying it. Nor is the former part of the assertion less false, than the latter is impious. That there should be ignorant Catholics is not wonderful, when we consider that they have been so long shut out from the means of knowledge, by the laws of their country. The higher ranks have been excluded from the benefits of our university, unless they renounced their religion; and what inducement could the man of lower station have to enter on the pursuit of knowledge, while the laws of the land forbad him to look up to the honor of a private tuition, or subordinate station in a public school. Yet under all these discouragements, the Catholics have refuted the charge of ignorance, and proved its falshood. Nay, they have lately exhibited specimens of knowledge, learning, and liberality, on reviewing which, their *accomplished* and *capable* calumniators should blush, and hide their heads.

However, my friends, this charge of *Catholic ignorance* and *incapacity* is only for *your* ears. The same lips convey to *them* a different tale. They are told, with great affection and regret, " that their abilities and their merits are well known ; and that they ought to share the benefits of the constitution in common with their brethren ; but that such is the ignorance, bigotry, and illiberality of a great majority of the Protestants, that nothing can be done for the Catholics, without offending *them*."

Now, who constitute this great majority of Protestants, not only in Ulster, but in Ireland ? *Presbyterians !* Are ye Presbyterians then, such *ignorant, bigotted,* and *illiberal wretches,* as those double-tongued tattlers, first attempt to *make,* and afterwards *represent* you ? With you it lies, either to justify or refute the charge. And be assured, such charge lies against you. I speak not on the authority of idle rumor. It has been made in my own hearing, again and again.

As the tale I have mentioned, is addressed to your folly, I shall now take notice of one addressed to your fears. Ye are told, that " the Catholics are combining against you, meditating the overthrow of our happy constitution, and preparing to embroil the nation in war."

This is as false as any part of the former. Notwithstanding the sage prognostications of our wise masters, all their proceedings are legal, orderly, and peaceful. And at this moment, they are supplicating—humbly and dutifully supplicating—his Majesty, for a redress of their grievances, and a share in the blessings of the constitution, which would bind them to their country, by interest as well as affection ; and they are looking, with imploring eye, for your intercessory voice in support of their prayer, which would unite them to *you* by ties of gratitude.

There is yet another suggestion, founded on, and addressed to, your jealousies and your interests. That is, " that the restoration of *their* rights and liberty would abridge or destroy *yours*."

This is absurdity too gross for any thing above idiotism, or childhood to swallow. Are your fields less fruitful, or your harvests less abundant, because those of your Catholic brethren share the benefits of the enlivening sun, refreshing showers, and dews of Heaven, in common with them? No! Nor would your liberties be injured, if slavery were banished from the earth; and, not only your Catholic brethren, but the whole human race, as free as ye are—or, *in justice ought to be*. Liberty, like the light of Heaven, though extended to infinity, is not diminished in its influence. No individual is deprived of its blessings, though ten thousand times ten thousand share them with him. He who tells you the contrary, may as well tell you, that " if the sun shine on Catholics, ye must pine in darkness;" or, " if the heathen be given Christ for a possession, ye must become out-casts from the family of God."

These are only a few of the political forgeries of the busy-body and slanderer, at this eventful moment. But they are such glaring instances of the baseness of his heart, and the venom of his tongue, that they could not be overlooked; especially in a case so nearly connected with your honor and your interest. And from their direct tendency to create alarm, jealousy, and distrust in the hearts of men, and consequently, weaken the confidence, endanger the peace, and destroy the comfort of society, I hope they will be sufficient to enforce the necessity of shutting your ears against every malicious tattler, and treating him and his fictions, with the contempt they deserve.

I meant to have mentioned some further improvement of the subject before us; but, as I fear I have already trespassed on your patience, I shall omit it for the present.

I shall, however, take the liberty of adding, that I have been thus diffuse, from the full conviction, that all I have said is implied in the subject before us—A subject, as important as ever employed the Song of Angel, or the tongue of man. And I have applied it to our present situation, because I am convinced it is my duty, when the ear of the ignorant and the simple is poisoned by falsehood, and their hearts envenomed by malicious insinuations—

When the oppreſſed Catholic is inflamed againſt the Preſbyterian, as the enemy of his rights, and oppoſer of his claims ; and the credulous Preſbyterian is made to fear that his throat is is about to be cut by the harmleſs Catholic, with whom he has lived in the habits of intimacy and goodwill, from his earlieſt infancy—when the public confidence is actually deſtroyed, by the groundleſs outcry, " that the public peace is in danger."

But believe me, my brethren, the public peace, and the *public purſe*, are in more danger from thoſe who originate ſuch alarms, than from *all the Catholics in the kingdom put together.* Who are they ?—I will tell you in few words who they are.—They are the official heirs and ſucceſſors of the very men, who, *leſs than ninety years ago*, repreſented to Queen Anne, that your forefathers were enemies to her government, and a dead weight on *their intereſts ;* that allowing them the rights of men, and the benefits of the conſtitution, would deſtroy both church and ſtate ; and who procured, by their outrageous clamour, the continuance of the infamous teſt-act, which excluded the Preſbyterians from every truſt, honor, and office of the ſtate, above that of a petty conſtable. At that period, every calumny was levelled againſt them which is now pointed at the Catholics ; and every alarm founded, which now diſturbs the public mind. And all this was done by a faction, which now arrogates the *lofty* title of *aſcendency*—by the placemen and penſioners of the day—by corrupt corporations, and a numerous body, whoſe office is ſo venerable, and name ſo ſacred, that it would be deemed impiety to mention them, with a venal train of ſycophants and expectants, gaping for the ſpoils of the public.

Let me now aſk you ; were the repreſentations of theſe men founded in truth ?—Ye know they were not ! And I now tell you, that the reports ſo induſtriouſly circulated, of danger from the Catholics, with which the weak and the ignorant are alarmed and terrified, are equally falſe. They are worſe than falſe—they are inſidious ! They are circulated, not only with a view to inflame your minds againſt your brethren, but to divert you from ſeeking—humbly and conſtitutionally ſeeking—that reform of government, which would deprive their authors of the ſpoils of oppreſſion ; but would raiſe your country to proſperity and happineſs !—A reform, without which the Catholics muſt continue ſlaves in their native land ; and ye—*even the proudeſt among you*—

have nothing left to boaſt of, but the excluſive honor of being *driven to market once in ſeven years*, and having your honor, your underſtanding, your conſcience, and your allegiance to your country, which ought to be ſacred, publicly diſpoſed of, by your lordly maſters : while your drivers are goaded on by ſome more powerful dependent on a foreign influence, which, behind the curtain of ſtate, manages the ſprings of your political puppet-ſhow.

To accompliſh this, national jealouſy, diſtruſt and diviſion are abſolutely neceſſary : and all theſe rumours are forged and circulated to excite and diffuſe them. Treat ſuch, therefore, with contempt. Let them not blind your underſtanding, biaſs your judgment, or corrupt your hearts, ſo as to inflame you againſt brethren, who deſire to be united with you, in order to ſwell that voice, with which ye demand your long-violated rights and liberties. Union is, not only the bond of peace, but the foundation of power, proſperity, and happineſs : and union can have no place between the perſecutor and the perſecuted, the oppreſſor and the oppreſſed, the tyrant and the ſlave. Let theſe diſtinctions then be done away ; and the evils we complain of will vaniſh with them. Say ye, with the firm, but reſpectful tone of free-born ſubjects, " they *ſhould* be done away, and the bleſſings of government extended with equal hand, to your long oppreſſed brethren." This, as I hope to prove on a future occaſion, it is my duty to inculcate, and yours to do. At preſent I ſhall only mention, that the relief to which it points, is the will of God ; and as we have devoted this day to religion, that it alone can render the ſervices of religion acceptable to him. " Is not this the faſt that I have choſen," ſaith the Lord, " to looſe the bands of wickedneſs, to undo the heavy burthens, to let the oppreſſed go free, and break every yoke ? If thou put away from the midſt of thee the yoke, the putting forth of the finger, and ſpeaking vanity : then ſhall thy light break forth as the morning, and thine health ſhall ſpring forth ſpeedily ; and thy righteouſneſs ſhall go before thee ; the glory of the Lord ſhall gather thee up. Then ſhalt thou call, and the Lord ſhall anſwer : Thou ſhalt cry, and he will ſay, here I am."

Let theſe bands of wickedneſs then be broken, which bind down our Catholic brethren to contempt, ſlavery, and wretchedneſs—Let their heavy burthens be undone, and their yoke broken :

then fhall the light of our profperity break forth as the morning ; the bleffing of God fhall unite us as brethren ; and we will have caufe, as far as *our* country is concerned, to celebrate the accomplifhment of that happy revolution, which Angels fung, in profpec only : " Glory to God, among the higheft—on earth peace — .odwill among men."

Preached to the Prefbyterian congregation of Portaferry, December 25, 1792.

SERMON III,

Tim. II. ʒ. 16, 17. *All Scripture is given by inspiration of God,
and is profitable for doctrine, for reproof, for correction, for instruction in righteousness ; that the man of God may be perfect, thoroughly furnished unto all good works.*

THAT all Scripture was given by inspiration of God, we
firmly believe. That it became neceffary, from the degeneracy
of man into ignorance, error, and fin ; that its defign was to
teach, reprove, correct, and inftruct him in righteoufnefs ; and
that it contains a perfect fyftem of precepts, the obfervance of
which would fecure his happinefs here, and lead him to happinefs
hereafter, we cannot deny.

In thefe particulars the chriftian world is nearly agreed : and
Proteftants have univerfally pleaded for, and fupported the principle, " that the Bible is the only infallible rule, both of faith
and practice."

This principle neceſſarily implies, that the doctrines and precepts of the Bible extend to, and comprehend every part of human duty, and every relation from which it ariſes ; and conſequently, that its principles, reproofs, and inſtructions, ſhould be applied for the correction of every error, and every ſin, which may lead him aſtray, or impair that happineſs to which wiſdom is the guide, and of which virtue is the parent, and religion the guardian.

This is ſo plain, that it cannot be diſputed ; and from it another conſequence directly follows. This is, that the more enormous any ſin is in itſelf, deſtructive in its tendency, or extenſive in its effects, the more it ought to be expoſed by the doctrines, and checked by the reproofs and corrections of religion.

In theſe principles and conſequences, conſidered as abſtract propoſitions, we are all agreed. Yet ſuch is the perverſeneſs of man—ſuch the partial attachment of every individual to his own prejudices, paſſions, and purſuits, that he thinks they ſhould be exempted from an univerſal law, and the denunciations of religion levelled againſt theſe ſins only, from which he is free.

This partiality, if indulged, would put an end to all reproof, correction, and inſtruction in righteouſneſs, reduce the Scriptures, though given by inſpiration, to an empty name, and leave inquity to range without reſtraint. Nay ! it would leave the ſovereignty of God over the conſcience and conduct of men, without an advocate, and remove all oppoſition to the increaſe and perpetuity of of Satan's kingdom. For ſo far as iniquity, of any kind, is ſuffered to paſs unnoticed, unreproved, and uncorrected—ſo far is the end of revelation defeated, the cauſe of Heaven abandoned, and the uſurpations of Satan, not only tolerated, but encouraged.

Hence, it is the duty of the Miniſters of religion, as watchmen of ſouls, ſtewards of the manifold grace of God, and guardians of truth and righteouſneſs, to obſerve errors and iniquities, as they riſe, to expoſe them in their deſtructive tendencies, to diſplay their enormity and guilt, and to reprove and correct them, with freedom and boldneſs. The commiſſions to the Prophets are one continued proof of this ; and the language of the Apoſtle Paul is, " Preach the word ; be inſtant, in ſeaſon,

out of feafon, exhort and reprove, with long-fuffering and doctrine; and rebuke with all authority."

That this preaching, exhortation, and reproof fhould extend
to every fin, and every tranfgreffion of the law of God, cannot
be denied. And that no rank, order, or office of men, is exempted from, or placed above them, I fhall afterwards prove, not
by doubtful difputations, but the decifive teftimony of the
word of God, and the facts it recites.

To an attentive mind it muft appear furprizing, that fuch proof
fhould be neceffary; as the very fuppofition, that any man is above
the reproof and correction of religion, or any action beyond their
reach, implies, that fuch man is above the authority of God, and
fuch action beyond the controul of his law.   Yet, that fuch proof
is neceffary, we cannot doubt, while the interference of religion and
its minifters is boldly condemned in the moft important concerns,
not only of life, but truth and juftice. Thefe are, where the duties of men, united in fociety, and placed in the relations of *governors* and *governed*, *magiftrates* and *people*, come under confideration.   Though all allow that the perfonal duties of temperance,
fobriety, and chaftity—that mutual love, fidelity, and order in families—and even juftice, truth, moderation, friendfhip, charity,
and peace, in a town or neighbourhood, fhould be recommended
and enforced, under the fanctions of religion; and every violation
of them expofed, reproved, and execrated with all the terrors of
damnation, though their effects are confined to individuals, or
extend only to a few families: yet, when power is abufed by governors, and thofe who act under them, to the purpofes of partiality, oppreffion, rapine, corruption, and violence, till whole nations are diftracted, plundered, and enflaved; and every right of
man prefumptuoufly trampled under-foot; the abettors of flavery
and corruption maintain, that religion fhould ftand by, as an idle
fpectator; and that all her exhortations, reproofs, and inftructi-
ons in righteoufnefs, fhould be buried in flavifh filence. In other
words, that religion and her minifters have no concern, either with
the duties or interefts of men, as members of a ftate; nor any
right to interfere with the conduct of rulers, and the affairs of
nations.

Groundlefs and abfurd as this pofition is, when applied to that
religion, of which God is the author, and the Bible the fta-

tute-book ; it muſt be admitted, as reſting on ſomething *like* ſolidity, in reſpect to political religious eſtabliſhment, created, protected, and ſupported by ſtates. Of theſe, kings are the head, policy the only principle, and political influence the end. For ſuch, therefore, to claim authority over rulers ; or their miniſters to expoſe, reprove, or correct the corruptions, uſurpations, or profligacy of governments, would be unpardonable preſumption, and political blaſphemy. Shall the creature ſay to the Creator, " I have power over thee ; thy ways are evil, and thy doings unjuſt ?" No, ſurely ! or ſhall the Prieſts and the Levites, who miniſter in the tabernacle of the ſtate, and was fat on the ſacrifices of the people's ſubſtance around its altars, lift up their voice againſt the oppreſſions, which raiſe them to ſeats among the Princes of the land ? This never *has* been the caſe—nor can it ever be ſuppoſed poſſible, till *principle become ſtronger than policy, and religion be reſcued from the mean drudgery of a political engine.* Till this period ſhall arrive, the voice of the prieſthood will be the echo of the Prince—his will their religion—his power the object of their ſlaviſh veneration—and the meaſures of government will be the ſtandard of devotion. The father of mercies will be ſolicited, *in preſcribed forms*, to become partner with the oppreſſor, the plunderer, and the aſſaſſin of nations ; and when iniquity, rapine, and bloodſhed proſper, Heaven's lofty arch will reſound with *impious* thankſgivings, and *blaſphemous* praiſe.

All this is natural and conſiſtent. As admirers of conſiſtency in others, let us, therefore, examine the religion, *not of the ſtate, but of the Bible*, that we may ſee what *it* teaches, and what conſiſtency requires of *us* who *profeſs* to believe it.

That *it* conſiders all men, *and of every rank*, as ſubject to its controul—that it directs its precepts *to all* ; and that it cenſures the violation of theſe *in all*, whether *princes, prieſts*, or *people*, I now *aſſert*, and ſhall endeavour to prove, not by doubtful diſputation, but as already mentioned, by the *deciſive teſtimony of the word of God, and the facts which it recites.*

The firſt fact to be adduced is ſo extenſive that it could not be compreſſed into the bounds of a ſermon. That is, that the great body of the Bible is almoſt entirely *political.* Of this, the prophetic writings, from beginning to end, are one continued teſtimony. They ſcarcely contain a ſingle exhortation, precept, promiſe, or threat, addreſſed to men as individuals, or members of a family; but as *ſtates* or *nations*. And whenever they deſcend to particulars, it is to denounce the tyranny of kings, the corruption of governments, and the *unprincipled* connivance and rapacity of Prieſts and Prophets. This is ſo plain, that any man who has read them, *if not more than half aſleep*, could not avoid ſeeing it. To them, therefore, *who can read*, I ſeriouſly recommend them. And if my recommendation is attended to, I am ſure the profit will more than repay the trouble; and the fact which I have mentioned, will appear undeniable.

The next fact is, " that the Bible interferes with affairs of government, by the precepts which it gives for directing the conduct both of magiſtrates and people, governors and governed, in the diſcharge of their political duties.

In proving this fact, I ſhall preſent you only with the language of the Bible; after one very ſhort obſervation reſpecting a cuſtom, in it alluded to.

In early ſtages of ſociety, magiſtrates are generally denominated, " the elders, or ancients of the people;" becauſe, before writing became general, and regular forms of education were introduced, old men, whoſe wiſdom was matured by experience, univerſally acted in that important character. And that juſtice might be ſpeedily adminiſtered in every city, which was, in itſelf a diſtinct ſtate, they ſat in the gates, from morning till night, to diſpenſe it to all, who went out and came in. Hence every precept in the Bible, commanding the " execution of judgment and juſtice in the gates," is to be conſidered, as *excluſively* directed to the governors and rulers of the people.

By this obſervation, ye are to examine and judge of the precepts and remarks which follow.

" Rob not the poor, becauſe he is poor; neither oppreſs the afflicted *in the gate*. For the Lord will plead their cauſe, and *ſpoil the ſoul* of thoſe who ſpoiled them. Take away the wicked from before the King, and his throne ſhall be eſtabliſhed in righteouſneſs. As a roaring lion, and a ranging bear, ſo is a wicked ruler over the poor people. The Prince, who wanteth underſtanding, is alſo a great oppreſſor. The King, by righteousness, establisheth the land; but he who receiveth gifts, over-throweth it. Scornful men bring a state into a snare; but wise men turn away wrath. If a ruler hearken to lies, all his servants will be wicked. The King, who *faithfully* judgeth the poor, his throne shall be established for ever. Open thy mouth, and judge righteously, and plead the cause of the poor and needy. Judges and officers shalt thou make thee, in *all thy gates*, throughout thy tribes; and they shall judge the people with just judgment. Thou shalt not wrest judgment; thou shalt not respect persons, neither take a gift. For a gift doth blind the eyes of the wife, and per-vert the words of the righteous. That which is *altogether* just thou shalt follow, *that thou mayest live, and inherit the land,* which the Lord thy God giveth thee."

" Hear the word of the Lord, ye rulers! Give ear unto the law of the Lord, ye people! Learn to do well, seek judgment, relieve the oppressed. Execute *true* judgment, and shew mercy and compassion, *every man to his brother,* and oppress not the stranger, nor the poor, and let none of you *imagine evil in his heart against his brother.* Speak ye the truth, every man to his neigh-bour, and execute the judgment *of peace and truth* in your gates."

These are a few of the general instructions of the Bible, which shew that religion prescribes the duty of Princes, as well as of the people. And from them we might safely conclude, that *her au-thority,* and *the duty of her teachers,* extend to both. However, we shall next see, that this conclusion does not rest on *general pre-cepts and remarks*; but that the Bible is prescribed *by God himself,* as the *standard* by which *Kings* are to *rule,* and *Princes govern*; and that it is the *duty* of the teachers of religion, where her *prin-ciples* are set aside, and her *precepts* violated, to " reprove, correct, and instruct in righteousness."

The first part of this position requires only one passage to esta-blish it immoveably. " When thou art come into the land, which the Lord thy God giveth thee, and shalt possess it, and shalt dwell therein, and shalt say, I will set a King over me, like as all the nations which are about me. It shall be, when he sitteth upon the throne of his kingdom, that he shall write him a copy of this law in a book, out of that which is before the Priests the Levites. And it shall be with him, and he shall read therein all the days of his life ; that he may learn to fear the Lord his God, to keep all the words of this law and thefe ftatutes, to do them—That his *heart be not lifted up above his brethren*, and *that he turn not afide from the commandment, to the right hand, or to the left* : to the end that he may prolong his days in his kingdom."

As this paffage is perfectly decifive, and eftablifhes beyond a doubt, the authority of the law of God over kings and governments ; we fhall now take notice of fome others, which enjoin the teachers of religion to reprove and correct their departure from its principles of eternal and immutable juftice ; and difplay the integrity, freedom, and boldnefs with which they difcharged their duty.

To this purpofe, the commiffion given to Jeremiah is perfectly in point. " Gird up thy loins, and arife, and fpeak unto them all that I command thee : Be not difmayed at their faces, left I confound thee before them. For, behold ! I have made thee this day a defenced city, and an iron pillar and brazen walls, againft the whole land, againft the *Kings* of Judah, againft the *Princes* thereof, againft the *Priefts* thereof, and againft the *People* of the land. And they fhall fight againft thee, but fhall not prevail ; for I am with thee, faith the Lord, to deliver thee."

The commiffion to Ifaiah is perfectly fimilar : " Cry aloud, fpare not ; lift up thy voice like a trumpet, and fhew my people their tranfgreffions, and the houfe of Jacob (the rulers of the people) their fins."

Ezekiel was fent to Pharaoh, king of Egypt, with denunciations againft his pride, oppreffion, and cruelty : And the following was his meffage to the rulers of Tyre : " Son of man, fay unto the Prince of Tyrus, thus faith the Lord God, becaufe thine heart is lifted up, and thou haft faid, I am a God, and fet thine heart as the heart of God, and haft defiled thy fanctuaries by the multitude of thine iniquities ; therefore, I will bring forth a fire from the midft of thee : it fhall devour thee : and I will bring thee to afhes upon the earth, in fight of all them that behold thee."

The commiffioners of the other Prophets are expreffed in like terms, and uniformly point to the fame objects : and the following

passages, among a multitude, demonstrate the honesty and boldness with which they discharged their duty.

" How is the faithful city become an harlot ? Righteousness
lodged in it, but now murderers : Thy Princes are become rebellious, and companions of thieves : Every one loveth gifts, and
followeth after rewards."

" As for my people, *children* are their oppressors, and *women*
rule over them. O my people, they, *who lead thee, cause thee to
err, and destroy the way* of thy paths. The Lord will enter into
judgment with the *rulers* of his people, and the *Princes* thereof : for
ye have eaten up the vineyard ; the *spoil of the poor* is in your
houses. *What mean ye,* that ye *beat my people to pieces, and grind
the faces of the poor ?*"

" Wo unto them, who *decree unrighteous decrees,* and write
grievousness which they have prescribed : *to turn aside the needy from
judgment,* and to *take away the right from the poor of my people*"

" Surely the Princes are become foolish ! the counsel of the
wise counsellors of Pharaoh is become brutish !"

" Wherefore hear the word of the Lord, *ye scornful men,* who
rule this people, which is in Jerusalem : because ye have said, we
have made a covenant with death, and with hell are we at agreement : When the overflowing scourge shall pass through, it shall
not come unto us ; for we have made *lies our refuge ;* and *under
falshood have we hidden ourselves.* Therefore, thus faith the Lord,
judgment will I lay to the line, and righteousness to the plummet,
and *the hail shall sweep away the refuge of lies,* and the waters shall o-
verflow the hiding-place. Your *covenant with death,* shall be *dis-
annulled,* and your *agreement with hell shall not stand.* When the
overflowing scourge shall pass through, *ye shall* be trodden down.
For *this is a people robbed* and *spoiled : They are for a prey, and none
faith, restore.*"

" Among my people are wicked men ; they lay wait, as they
who set snares—they set a trap—they *catch men.* As a cage is
full of birds, so are their houses full of deceit : therefore, *they
are become great and waxen rich. They are waxen fat—they shine !*
Yea, they overpass the deeds of the wicked. They judge not the

caufe of the fatherlefs, yet they profper ; and the caufe of the needy do they not judge. Thefe are the men who *devife mifchief*, give *wicked counfel in the ftate.*"

" Behold the Princes of Ifrael ! every one within thee are fet to fhed blood. In the midft of thee have they dealt by oppref-fion. In thee are men who carry tales to fhed blood. In thee they have taken gifts ; and thofe haft greedily gained of thy neighbours by extortion. Thy Princes are like wolves ravening for prey. The people of the land have ufed oppreffion, and exercifed robbery ; and have vexed the poor and needy."

" Hear this, O Priefts ! Hearken, ye houfe of Ifrael ! and give ear, O houfe of the King ! *execute judgment in* the gates."

" Hear this, ye that fwallow up the needy, even to make the poor of the earth fail. Woe to the bloody city ! it is full of lies and robbery : the prey departeth not. The Princes within her, are roaring lions : her judges are ravening wolves. Spoiling and vio-lence are before me ; and there are that *raife up ftrife and contenti-on.* Therefore, the law is flacked, and judgment doth never go forth, for the wicked doth compafs the righteous. The Prince demandeth, and the judge afketh for reward ; and the *great man* uttereth his *mifchievous defire : fo they wrap it up among them !* none calleth for juftice, nor any pleadeth for truth. They truft in va-nity, and fpeak lies. They conceive mifchief, and bring forth iniquity. The act of violence is in their hands. Their feet run to evil, and they make hafte to fhed innocent blood. Their thoughts are thoughts of iniquity ; wafting and deftruction are in their paths. The way of peace they know not. Therefore is judgment far from us ; neither doth juftice overtake us. We wait for light, but behold, obfcurity : for brightnefs, but we walk in darknefs. We roar all like bears ; and mourn like fore doves : We look for judgment, but there is none—for *deliverance*, but it is far from us. Judgment is turned away backwards, and juftice ftandeth afar off : truth is fallen in the ftreet, and iniquity cannot enter. Yea, *truth faileth ;* and *he, who departeth from evil, is ac-counted mad.* And the Lord faw it ; and it difpleafed him that there was *no judgment.*"

The fcenes exhibited in thefe few paffages, are equally affecting and inftructive. They prefent us with a melancholy picture of the depravity of rulers, and the abuses of government : and at the same time, they clearly prove both the *right* and *duty* of the teachers of religion to reprove their tyranny, oppression, and cruelty ; and display the integrity and boldness with which that duty was discharged.

Taking it for granted, that they are sufficient for these purposes, I shall now proceed one step further, and shew, that by virtue of their office, they are likewise to enforce the abolition of these oppressions, penalties and pains, which former governments have inflicted, and still continue in force.

" Touching the house of the King of Judah, say, hear ye the word of the Lord, O house of David ; thus saith the Lord, execute judgment in the morning, remove your exactions from my people, and *deliver him that is spoiled out of the hands of the oppressor ;* lest my fury go out like fire, and burn that none can quench it, *because of the evil of your doings.*"

" Thus saith the Lord, go down to the King of Judah and say ; hear the word of the Lord, O King of Judah, *thou,* and *thy servants,* and *thy people,* execute judgment and righteousness, and deliver the spoiled out of the hand of the oppressor : do no wrong, nor violence, nor shed innocent blood."

These sayings were addressed, *not to the rulers only,* but to *the people* also ; plainly shewing that they had a *right,* and that it was their *duty* to interfere in behalf of the oppressed ; and on the hardest supposition, to *petition for their relief.* And as the indolence of the people, and the fear of incurring difficulties, frequently prevent their doing right, and induce them to plead ignorance, in excuse for their neglect, the following passage may be quoted with great propriety. " If thou forbear to deliver them that are drawn unto death, and those that are ready to be slain : If thou say, behold ! we knew it not : doth not he, who knoweth the heart, consider it : And he, who keepeth the soul, doth he not know it ? And shall he not render to every one according to his deeds ?"

The following examples extend farther still—they go to prove the interference of the teachers of religion, by the command of God, not only with the conduct of rulers in respect to the people ; but the conduct of Kings and kingdoms to each other.

Rehoboam, having raifed an hundred and eighty thoufand men, to make war againft Jeroboam, to which the ten tribes had revolted, was prevented by the interference of Shemaiah, a Prophet.

Three years afterwards, Shifhak, King of Egypt, marched againft Jerufalem, with a prodigious army ; and as the facred hiftorian informs us, " becaufe they had tranfgreffed." Shemaiah again interpofed, and *charged the King and Princes with their iniquities ;* on which they reformed, and Judah was faved from deftruction.

Afa, King of Judah, bribed Benhadad of Syria, to break a league with the king of Ifrael, for which Hanani, the Seer, feverely rebuked him, and charged him with foolifhnefs.

Jehofhaphat, King of Judah, *reproved* and *inftructed* by Jehu, fon of Hanani, vifited his kingdom, reformed his government, and charged the judges of the land to avoid partiality and oppreffion. The principle on which he enforced the charge, deferves particular attention. " Take heed," fays he, " what ye do ; for ye judge, *not for man, but for the Lord, who is prefent in the judgment.*"

Eliezer reproved Jehofhaphat, for joining with Ahaziah, King of Ifrael, in an unjuft war againft Tarfhifh.

Amaziah, King of Judah, hired an hundred thoufand mercenaries, for which he paid an hundred talents of filver, (about 36,000l.) to make war againft the Edomites : but on the remonftrance of a Prophet, he difmiffed the fanguinary hirelings, and forfeited the money.

And when Ifrael, having prevailed over Judah in an oppreffive war, took two hundred thoufand women and children captives, and purpofed to keep them in flavery ; Oded, a Prophet of the Lord, thus addreffed them : " The Lord God of your fathers was wroth with Judah, and hath delivered them into your hands ; and now ye propofe to keep under the children of Judah and Jerufalem, for *bond-men* and *bond-women* unto you. But are thefe not with, *even with you,* fins againft the Lord your God ? Now, *hear me,* therefore, and *deliver up the captives again,* which ye have taken captive of your *brethren; for the fierce wrath of the Lord is upon you."*

The Princes immediately held a council, and in obedience to the united voice of religion and humanity, enforced the Prophet's words. Their address to the army deserves to be engraven on every heart. " They said unto the people, ye shall not bring in the captives hither : for, whereas we have offended against the Lord already, ye intend to add to our sins and our trespass ; for our trespass is great, and there is fierce wrath against Israel." Nor are the sensibility, religion, and generosity of the people less remarkable. They instantly sacrificed their ambition and their covetousness at the shrine of humanity, truth, and justice. " They released the captives and the spoil, before the Princes and all the congregation. And they rose up and took the captives, *and clothed all that were naked among them, and arrayed them, and shod them, and gave them to eat and to drink, and anointed them, and carried all the feeble of them upon asses, and brought them to Jericho, to their brethren !!!"*

Glorious men ! blessed ! every blessed be your memory, and your example sacred ! But blush, ye *pretended* disciples of a merciful Jesus, equally strangers to *its* influence, and the benign spirit of your exalted master ! who rejoice in the slavery of your brethren, and glory in their debasement ! Hide your heads, ye devoted minions of tyranny and oppression, who pledge your despicable lives, and your fortunes, to perpetuate corruption, and entail wretchedness on generations unborn !

But I forbear the reflections which the case sugests. Let us confine our attention to the fact which it goes to establish, in common with the others which I have quoted : that is, " that it is the office of religion, and its teachers, to expose, reprove, and correct, the partiality, oppression, and tyranny of rulers ; and even the *unprincipled combinations* and *iniquitous transactions* of kings with kings, and nations with nations."—A fact, not only founded on the law of God, but uniformly supported by the conduct of his inspired prophets—A fact so evident, from the passages produced, that he who denies it, need not blush to deny, that light shines around him, or the earth supports his steps.

Religion, however, carries her authority still farther ; and the conduct of the Prophets will justify mankind in the exercise of it.

As this will appear afterwards, I shall now consider two cavils which ignorance or perverseness may, perhaps, bring forward against me.

I have mentioned *the Bible*, as the standard by which we were to ascertain, whether religion has a controul over the conduct of Kings, and the measures of government.

Now, perhaps, it may be alledged that the law of Moses alone, as contained in the five books ascribed to him, is concerned in this question; this law being alluded to, as the standard in all the following books.

This law I shall readily admit as the *standard* by which governments were to be regulated. As such, it not only prescribes the rules of impartial justice, moderation, and integrity, by which Kings were to govern; but teaches, that the observance of these was *the condition* on which they should be continued in power. For this is the evident meaning of the words; " that he may *prolong his days in his kingdom*."

This law, therefore, may be considered as a *fixed constitution*, by which government was to be framed and regulated, and rulers directed in the discharge of their duty. Hence, the judges and Kings of Israel were enjoined to have a copy of it *continually* with them, " that they might keep all the words and statutes thereof, to do them. And, has been observed, the keeping and doing these was the condition on which their power was to be prolonged.

These statutes they frequently violated, by treachery, oppression, and cruelty; and the records of following times, specifying their crimes, and the steps taken by the Prophets to correct and reform them, previous to their deposition, banishment, or death, shew the manner of procedure which ought to be adopted in all such cases. And the instances I have quoted, are so many *statutes on the case*, proposed as precedents *by divine authority*, for the imitation of all ages.

These records were, at different periods, committed to writing; and were collected by Ezra, after the return from the Babylonish captivity, about one thousand and fifty years after the giving of the law. From that time they were publicly adopted, as a *divine rule.* Our Saviour and his Apostles, acknowledged, quoted, and appealed to them *as such.* *They* are the *Scriptures,* all the parts of which the Apostle Paul declares, in our text, " to be given by inspiration of God ; and to be profitable, for doctrine, for reproof, for correction, for instruction in righteousness ; that the man of God may be perfect, *thoroughly* furnished unto all good works :" and of which he declares elsewhere, " that the facts contained in them, were *our examples,*", and written for *our admonition,* on whom the ends of the world are come."

Now, in what sense were they written for admonition ? or, in what manner can they be profitable for doctrine, reproof, correction, and instruction in righteousness, but by teaching us to avoid the evil forbidden and condemned ; and to practise the good recommended, whether by precept or example ? None possible that I can discover ! !

Let me now ask you ; are not the passages, which I have quoted, part of these records which were written for our admonition ; and do they not contain part of these examples, which are holden out to us ? most assuredly.—And do not these *admonitions* and *examples* clearly shew, " that the interference of the teachers of religion, to reprove, correct, and denounce the injustice, fraud, and oppression of rulers, and the depravity and corruption of governments, is sanctioned by *the law of God,* and the uniform declarations and example of *all* the Prophets ? and that *their* conduct is proposed to us, *as objects of imitation,* by Christ and his Apostles. No christian dare deny it.

Hence, then, I conclude, that not only the *right,* but the *duty* of the teachers of religion to expose, reprove, and correct *every action, and every measure* contrary to the *eternal principles* of truth and justice, rests on the broad basis of the Bible.—Whether such actions, and such measures, be done and pursued, by *prince* or *people, governors* or *governed, states* or *individuals.*

The second cavil may be, " that the exhortations, reproofs, corrections, and instructions, in the passages I have quoted, were not pronounced by the ordinary teachers of religion ; but by persons inspired, and sent for the special purpose :" and there-

H

fore, " that the acts performed by them, came not within the office of *ordinary* religious teachers."

This I chearfully admit, in its full force, *so far as it states a fact*: but I deny the conclusion drawn from it, and hope *clearly* to refute it.

We have seen, that partiality, injustice, fraud, oppression, and cruelty in rulers, were *strictly* forbidden by the law.—We know that the Priests were the guardians and teachers of that law—Is it not evident then, that *in the strictest* sense, the teaching, nay, the *very reading* of it was a direct censure of these enormities ?—But it is said, " the teachers did not censure them." I grant it ! but the conclusion from this is ; " not that such censure was foreign from their duty ;" but, " that in neglecting it, they neglected their duty, and betrayed their trust." Would to God ! they stood alone, to bear the weight of this heavy charge !

I know to many it may seem bold, and I am sure it is melancholy. But it is not more bold or melancholy, than it is true. The corruption, neglect, and depravity of the Priests, gave rise to the necessity of sending extraordinary Prophets, for the purpose of correcting these enormities. The Priests had become sharers in the spoils of oppression, and accomplices in its guilt ; and consequently *deaf* to the word of the Lord, and *dumb* in the discharge of their duty. Attend to what follows, and judge for yourselves !

" The watchmen of Israel are blind—they are *all* ignorant—they are dumb dogs—they cannot bark ; dreaming, lying down, loving to slumber. Yea, they are *greedy* dogs, which can never have enough ; they all look to their own ways, *every one for his gain.* Come ye, say they, I will fetch wine, and we will fill ourselves with strong drink ; for to-morrow shall be as this day, and much more abundant."

" The Priests said not, where is the Lord ? And they who handle the law, knew me not ; the pastors also have transgressed against me. From the Prophet, even to the Priest, every one dealeth falsely. Is this house, which is called by my name, become a den of thieves in your eyes ?"

" Both Prophet and Prieſt are prophane ; yea, in mine houſe have I found their wickedneſs, ſaith the Lord. I have ſeen alſo, in the Prophets of Jeruſalem, an horrible thing ! They walk in lies ; they ſtrengthen alſo the hands of evil-doers, that none doth return from his wickedneſs. They bite with their teeth, and cry peace ; and he that putteth not into their mouths, they even prepare war againſt him !"

" There is a conſpiracy of her Prophets in the midſt of her, like a roaring lion ravening the prey. They have devoured ſouls ; they have taken the treaſure and precious things. The Prieſts have violated my law, and profaned my holy things : They have put no difference between the holy and profane ; neither have they ſhewed difference between the unclean and the clean : and from them, profaneneſs is gone forth into all the land."

What a dreadful picture is here preſented to the eye ! A picture, ſurcharged with the odious colourings of ignorance, indolence, rapacity, and drunkenneſs ; fraud, perverſion of the law, profaneneſs, falſehood, and treachery ! When we review this picture, as the faithful repreſentation of the prieſthood, can we be ſurpriſed, that they were ſilent concerning the enormities of the rulers, which it was their duty to reprove ? or the oppreſſions of the people, on whoſe ſpoils they revelled ?—At the miſſion of extraordinary teachers who were to ſupply their neglects ? or, the inſtructions to the Prophets, who were to plead the cauſe of the people ? " Feed the flock of the ſlaughter," ſaith the Lord, " whoſe poſſeſſors ſlay them, and hold themſelves not guilty : and they who ſell them, ſay, bleſſed be the Lord ! I am rich : and their own ſhepherds pity them not. They eat the fat, and clothe themſelves with the wool ; they kill them that are fed, but feed not the flock. The diſeaſed they have not ſtrengthened, neither that which was ſick : they have not bound up the broken, nor brought back that which was driven away, neither ſought that which was loſt : but with force, and with cruelty have they ruled them. Thus ſaith the Lord God, wo be to the ſhepherds of Iſrael, who feed themſelves ! Should not the ſhepherds feed the flock ? Wo unto the fooliſh ſhepherds who follow their own ſpirit, and have ſeen nothing ! O Iſrael, thy Prophets are like foxes in the deſert. They have ſpoken vanity, and divine lies ! ſaying, peace where there was no peace : therefore ſhall mine hand be upon them : they ſhall not be in the aſſembly of my people, neither shall they be written in the writing of the house of Israel: and ye shall know that I am the Lord."

Though these passages are sufficient, not only to obviate the cavil I have mentioned, but to account for the silence of the established teachers of religion; and add stability to the fact, " that it was their duty to have exposed, reproved, and corrected the prevailing enormities of rulers, and corruptions of government," I shall add another, which places the matter in a light still clearer.

" A wonderful and horrible thing is committed in the land! The Prophets prophesy falsely, and the Priests bear rule by their means; and my people love to have it so!"

Here we see the falsehood of the Prophets was subservient to the ambition and aggrandisement of the Priests. By their means the people were blinded, and the Priests promoted to places of authority and power among their brethren. In this case, we cannot be surprised, that they should slumber over the law, and be silent in behalf of the oppressed. But that such falsehoods should be pleasing to the people, whose oppressions they were calculated to multiply and confirm, at first view, is somewhat wonderful! Yet, so it was: " the people loved to have it so."

The fact is, man is the creature of habit, and the slave of his own indolence and fears. By long custom he may be reconciled to any thing. And when once sunk into corruption, and pressed down into insignificance, all his powers of mind become enfeebled, and his sentiments perverted. The difference between right and wrong, dignity and meanness, honor and shame, is scarcely felt. To manly exertion he is a professed enemy. And at last, he becomes so totally debased, that truth itself is disagreeable. His only pleasure is, to hear the delusive fictions which flatter his insignificance, and masque his crimes. These he loudly calls for, and swallows with greediness; while he rejects with abhorrence, the sacred and salutary truths which recall him to his proper character, the assertion of his rights, and the recovery of his native dignity.

The address of the most high, by the Prophet Isaiah, to his people, thus sunk into meanness, corruption, and depravity, is striking and awful. " Go," said he, " write it before them in a table, and note it in a book, that it may be, for the time to come, for ever and ever ; that this is a rebellious people, lying children —children who will not hear the law of the Lord: who say to the seers, see not ; and to the Prophets, prophesy not to us right things. Speak unto us smooth things : Prophesy deceits. Wherefore, thus saith the Lord, because ye despise this word, and trust in oppression and perversion, and depend thereon ; this iniquity shall be to you as a breach ready to burst, a swelling in an high wall, whose breaking cometh suddenly, at an instant."

From the passages brought together on this subject, the following particulars appear plain and undeniable :

I. The controul of religion over governors, governments and nations.

II. Not only the right, but the duty of teachers, to expose, reprove, and censure, the partiality,, oppression, and tyranny of rulers, the destructive influence of evil counsellors, and the corruption of governments.

III. That this duty extends, not only to the concerns of magistrates and people—governors and governed, but to leagues, treaties, and combinations of Kings with Kings, and nations with nations, for the purpose of injustice, oppression, and bloodshed. And,

IV. It has come to light, as by accident, from several of the passages I have quoted, that the necessity of sending extraordinary Prophets, to reprove and correct political fraud, oppression, and violence ; and thereby, prevent national ruin, arose from the ignorance, indolence, covetousness, and profligacy of a worthless priesthood ; and the meanness, obstinacy, and folly of a silly people, who preferred flattery and delusion to the law of the Lord, and the words of truth, soberness, and a sound mind.

These facts, thus fully substantiated, being evident from the holy scriptures, which, as the Apostle tells us, " were given by inspiration, written for our admonition, and useful for doctrine, reproof, correction, and instruction in righteousness ;" I shall now shew that religion carries her authority farther still ; and that the Bible teaches us other doctrines equally important.

I. It teaches us, that as it is the duty of the teachers of religion to rebuke the partiality, injustice, and oppression of governors, and expose the abuses of government; so it is the duty of the people to call for and enforce reform.

II. That where any particular body, or description of men labours under partial grievances, hardships, or oppressions in a state, it is not only the duty of the existing government to redress and remove them; but where they may neglect such redress, or refuse it to the dutiful petition and remonstrance of the aggrieved, it is the duty of their brethren and fellow-subjects to espouse their cause, and support their claims, by every fair and justifiable mean.

In support of these lessons, I shall only recall your attention to two or three sentences of what I have already quoted.

" Wo unto them who decree unrighteous decrees, and write grievousness, which they have prescribed; that is, who enact partial, unjust, and oppressive laws; to turn aside the needy from judgment, and to take away the right from the poor of my people."

" Hear the word of the Lord, O King of Judah, thou, and thy servants, and thy people, deliver the spoiled out of the hand of the oppressor, loose the bands of wickedness, undo the heavy burdens, and break every yoke: give ear unto the law of the Lord ye people; learn to do well, seek judgment, relieve the oppressed. Take away the wicked from before the king; and his throne shall be established in righteousness."

Here we see, that the commands, " seek judgment, relieve the oppressed, and take away the wicked from before the king," were directed, not only to the Prince and his servants, but to the people: And in the words which follow, the displeasure of the Lord is expressed against them, because they did not demand of their rulers the restoration of their brethren to their rights and liberties, and a reform of the government, which took away, and with-held them. " This is a people robbed and spoiled! They are for a prey, and none saith restore. None calleth for justice, nor any pleadeth for truth: and the Lord was displeased, because there was no judgment."

These lessons, equally plain and important, are for the direction of every nation, and the inftruction of all people, who believe the bible. It cannot be wrong, therefore, for us to learn, know, and practife them. Would to God, we had no occafion to apply them!

This, however, is not the cafe! Wifely as our government was originally conftructed, and folidly founded in the principles of juftice, and the rights of men; yet in the lapfe of ages, it has been removed from its original foundation, perverted in its principles, deranged in its ftructure, and converted to a mif-fhapen and monftrous pile of venality, corruption, and partiality!

That this is the cafe, requires no proof. The whole kingdom has long feen, and feverely felt it. Nay, minifters have not only avowed it, but pleaded the neceffity of corrupt influence for its fupport.

In conformity with this avowal, taxes are multiplied, and increafed to fuch a degree, that the price of many articles, of moft extenfive confumption; and which, from habit, have become almoft neceffaries of life, is nearly doubled during the laft ten years. And to what purpofe? Not to fupport an army for the defence of the country! Thank God! we have no need of fuch. The genius of the country is roufed; and its arm ftrung for its own defence!—Not to provide a fleet to protect our coafts, fhould danger threaten us!—Not to maintain the execution of law; or fubftantially promote agriculture, manufactures and commerce! No.—But to bribe the nominal reprefentatives of one part of the people, to betray them, and make a prey of the whole—to fupport a burthenfome, unprincipled, and imperious train of ufelefs placemen, and beggarly penfioners—a voracious national poor lift! whofe lufts are infatiable, " whofe teeth are as fwords, and their jaw-teeth as knives, to devour the oppreffed from off the earth, and the needy from among men!" And we have lately heard venal and oppreffive corporations, and felf-devoted factions, in almoft every county of the kingdom, proclaiming this corruption and oppreffion, which they blafphemoufly call our conftitution, the delight of their hearts; and pledging their lives and fortunes to fupport them.

In thefe circumftances, the nation could fee no profpect of relief, or fafety, but in a radical reform, which would remove all these evils, or a total revolution. From a just view of the convulsions and horrors which attend revolutions, and a conviction that nothing but incorrigible despotism, and dire necessity, can justify the experiment, they have wisely determined, in obedience to the call of duty, to look for, and demand reform. And though " oppression sometimes makes wise men mad ;" they have proceeded with temper, moderation, and order. Though " the multitude of their grievances has obliged them to complain, and the arm of the mighty to cry out ;" the voice of sedition has not been heard, nor the hand of intemperance and riot raised up. A solemn dignity has marked their steps ; and the genius of the land has led them to demand the re-establishment of government on the principles of our happy constitution, of which the people's rights are the foundation, their will the law, and their happiness the end. And to their immortal honor, they have determined to seek, pursue, and obtain this great object, not by force or tumultuous violence, but by the wise and rational means which the constitution itself prescribes and sanctions—that is, by calling the people together, to consult coolly and deliberately on this interesting subject, that the public sentiment may be known, by free communication, and the public will concentered in a point, from which its expression may flow, with clearness, harmony, and strength into the houses of parliament, and the presence of majesty.

In this all seem to be agreed, except those who feed on the spoils of the poor, and wax fat by oppression ; and those, who for reasons best known to themselves, have resigned their principles or spirit to express them to some lordly leader.

To the former of these, the voice of religion, and the calls of duty need not be directed. To these their ears have been long shut, and their hearts insensible. The latter, however, would do well to consider the words of the Prophet Isaiah, and the wise Solomon. " The leaders of this people cause them to err ; and they who are led of them, are destroyed. Him who saith to the wicked, thou art righteous, will the people curse ;—nations shall abhor him. But to them who rebuke him, shall be delight ; and a good blessing shall come upon them."

That the method proposed for obtaining reform, is the way of peace, as well as of prudence, every attentive mind must see. If pursued with unanimity and discretion, it must terminate in happineſs. If not, " confuſion and every evil work" may be reaſonably expected from the preſent agitation of the public mind, and the provocations which have occaſioned it. And ſhould diviſion among the people tempt government to reject requiſitions, founded in right, and ſanctioned by religion, " to looſe the bands of wickedneſs, and break the yoke of oppreſſion," ſomething more expreſſive than requiſition may be juſtly dreaded ; and He alone, whoſe eye looks forward through the infinity of ages, can pronounce upon the iſſue ; while they, whoſe tyranny, or connivance with tyranny, has provoked the public paſſions, muſt bear the guilt, and anſwer for the conſequences.

The other leſſon, of which I took notice, as recommended to our attention, by a variety of the paſſages cited, ariſes from the debaſement and oppreſſion of part of a nation, by laws unjuſt in their principle, and partial in their operation. Where this is the caſe, we have clearly ſeen, that God has commanded their brethren to petition in their behalf ; or, as it is expreſſed in ſcripture, " to plead their cauſe ;" and ſay to their oppreſſors, RESTORE.

Does this leſſon—dictate of pure humanity—and clothed with the authority of God, apply to us ? Moſt aſſuredly ! like all the other parts of ſcripture, it was written " for our inſtruction in righteouſneſs ;" and carries with it, in our caſe, ſevere reproof, and well-earned correction. Sorry I am, that it has ſo long, like many other leſſons of the bible, been neglected, deſpiſed, and trampled under-foot, by the prevalence of prejudice, paſſion, and political faction. For never were partiality and injuſtice more conſpicuous on earth, than they have been in the land of our nativity, for upwards of ſixty years. Not a ſmall part—but three fourths of its inhabitants—the great body of the people—have been reduced to the moſt abject and humiliating ſervitude ; excluded from every office, honor, truſt, and emolument of the ſtate, which they uniformly ſupported by their induſtry, and enriched by their commerce ; not only denied, but declared incapable of real property : taxed in parliament, grand juries, and veſtries, without conſent, perſonal or repreſentative ; excluded from every means of inſtruction, yet reproached and puniſhed for their ignorance ; deprived of the protection of the law, by being excluded from ſerving on juries ; and prohibited the uſe of arms for the ſafety of their naked and defenceleſs perſons.

I

The circumstances of this degradation render it as odious as it is intolerable. These are marked, not only with cruelty and injustice, but national perfidy. By the treaty of Limerick, on the faith of which the Roman Catholics of Ireland submitted to King William in 1691, they were to be secured in the enjoyment of rights and privileges, therein specified or alluded to. This treaty was signed by his Majesty's commander of the army, and the Lords Justices of Ireland, confirmed by the King and Queen, under the great seal of England, solemnly ratified afterwards by an act of parliament, and continued inviolate for thirty-six years. During this period, they enjoyed the privileges, and exercised the rights guaranteed to them; those of serving on juries, and voting for members of parliament, not excepted; nor did they incur the slightest imputation of disloyalty, or disaffection to government, from their bitterest enemies, though alarms of invasion were repeatedly spread, and a neighbouring nation convulsed by rebellion.

Yet in the year 1727, without fault or provocation on their part, the parliament chosen by them, in common with their protestant brethren, stripped them of every power and privilege of freemen, and in particular, left them incapable of joining in the election of another. Under all the incapacities which this and succeeding parliaments created, they continued till within these few years; and even now, the greatest and most opprobrious lie heavy upon them.

Yet still it is remarkable, that during these sixty-five years of worse than Egyptian slavery, in which insult and ignomy have frequently added to oppression, they have never forfeited, by act or declaration, their character of unshaken loyalty to their King, and respectful obedience to government—that very government which reduced them to slavery, poverty, and wretchedness, and out-transubstiating transubstantiation, continues to convert their flesh into bread, and their blood into wine, for communicants in iniquity. Nay, though rebellion again raised her head in a sister kingdom during that period; and we have had repeated wars with the nation, to whose humanity they owe what their hearts hold dearest, they have fought the battles of their country against her, both by sea and land! And on a late occasion, when the kingdom was robbed of the defence for which it liberally paid, for a purpose which policy disclaimed, humanity reprobated, and Hea-

ven had defeated—When the fleets of that nation rode triumph-
ant on our coasts, and government declared that protection rested
with ourselves; instead of resentment or cold indifference, they
caught the patriotic flame which animated the kingdom, and
gave birth to an army of citizen-soldiers, unequalled in the records
of the world. And though ye, in the hour of your darkness, rejected them from your ranks; be it known unto you, that in the
other parts of the kingdom, they formed an important part of that
illustrious body, who generously stood forward for the defence of
their brethren—who received the united and well-earned thanks
of King, Lords, and Commons, for the salvation of their country—and who shall live in the grateful remembrance of posterity,
and admiration of the world, in spite of pithless proclamations,
till the Angel of God shall proclaim; " arise ye dead, and come
to judgment." Nay, at this very moment, though the last voice
which the patient, though oppressed, people heard, from the abettors of their oppressions, was fraught with the provoking accents;
" your claims are seditious; your hopes groundless, and your
petitions vain—ye shall bear our chains for ever; and our yoke
shall gall the necks of your posterity, to the end of the world"—
At this moment, I say they are humbly supplicating a reversal of
the stern decree, and praying from man, a restoration of the rights,
which they received from God.

This is not a picture, but a faint sketch of their grievances,
their patience, and their patriotism. And when ye consider their
degraded situation; the injustice and perfidy which reduced them
to it; the length of time, through which it has been continued
from father to son; the dutiful and loyal part which they have
uniformly acted; and the offers of lives and fortunes which have
been lately made to keep them in eternal degredation and wretchedness; I trust you will feel yourselves called upon—irresistably
called upon—by the united voice of religion, justice, and humanity, to join your intercessory voice with the language of their
petion; " to plead the cause of the oppressed; to deliver the
spoiled from the hand of the oppressor; and shew mercy and
compassion, every man to his brother; least the fury of the Lord
go out like fire, and burn that none can quench it, because of
the evil of your doings."

Thus, I hope, I have fully established the assertion with which
I set out, in all its parts, both as it respects religion and her

teachers. I have fhewn that her controul, and their duty extends to every rank of men ; and their exhortations, reproofs, and corrections to every violation of the law of God.

As this is denied, principally in refpect to governors and ftates, I have produced a regular chain of evidence, in direct oppofition to fuch denial.——Evidence, which clearly proves, that the fins of kings and people, governors and governed, ftates and individuals, come equally under their reproofs and corrections——Nay, proves that if politics, in the only proper fenfe of the word, are to be excluded from the pulpit, the greater part of the bible muft be excluded with them.

I have likewife pointed out, by the paffages quoted, thofe political fins, which religion moft exprefsly condemns, and commands her teachers to expofe, reprove, and endeavour to correct ; together with the means which they ufed for effecting their reform.

I have farther confidered the leffons, which we ought to learn and practice, from thefe paffages of holy writ ; and applied them to our own affecting fituation.

And you will obferve, that I have not, through the whole, admitted one confideration of human policy, or one principle of worldly wifdom, into what I have laid before you. I have only reprefented the principle laid down, and the duty arifing from it, as they are founded in, and fupported by the word of God. How far the adoption of the one, and the performance of the other, may affect the petty interefts of this or the other political party, or the views of fcheming monopolifts, in politics, ftate-religion, manufactures, or commerce, I have left to the plodding ftatefman, the mercenary worldling, and the interefted partizan to determine. That the principle is true, the leffons juft, and the duties real, is enough for me. And that they are fo, cannot be denied, if the bible fpeaks truth.

In the full conviction of this, I have laid the whole freely before you. What may be the effect, I leave with you, and Him who fearcheth the heart, whofe eye is upon you.

That fome may be offended with me I cannot doubt. The oppreſſors of the earth, and the abettors of oppreſſion, partiality, and rapine, with the whole train of the bigotted, the illiberal, and the corrupt, were offended with thoſe who firſt ſpoke the words, by the command and inſpiration of God, which I have now repeated. Micaiah was inſulted, and impriſoned; Jeremiah threatened with death for attempting to reform and ſave his country; the Apoſtles perſecuted for ſpeaking the truth; and, what ſhould weigh more than ten thouſand examples, the bleſſed Jeſus was accuſed of rebellion, by a blind-led, ſeditious, and head-ſtrong multitude, and crucified as a blaſphemer. Why, then ſhould I be ſurpriſed, if all ſuch be offended with me? I will not be ſurpriſed; neither will I be afraid. Firm, " as an iron pillar, or wall of braſs," I'll ſtand erect, to declare the truth of the bible, and enforce your duty, while God vouchſafes me underſtanding to know, an heart to feel, and a tongue to expreſs them.

On the other hand, I know many will be pleaſed and gratified. Let me only intreat ſuch, that their pleaſure may not terminate, like that of the people of Iſrael, as deſcribed by the Lord, to the Prophet Ezekiel. " Son of man, the children of thy people ſpeak one to another, every one to his brother, ſaying, Come, I pray you, and hear what is the word that cometh forth from the Lord. They come unto thee, as the people cometh; and they ſit before thee, as my people; and they hear thy words, but they will not do them; for with their mouth they ſhew much love; but their heart goeth after their covetouſneſs. And lo! thou art unto them as a very lovely ſong, of one that hath a pleaſant voice, and can play well on an inſtrument: for they hear thy words, but they do them not."

Preached to the Preſbyterian Congregation of Portaferry, January 13, 1793.

ERRATA.

Page 3, line 2, from the bottom, for "loves" read "loaves." P. 4, l. 18, for "claims" r. "chains." P. 6, l. 1, before "prejudices" r. "whose" P. 7, l. 18, after "all" infue "its." P. 8, l. 9, for "induced" r. "endued." P. 9, l. 21, for "fanctified," r. "fanctioned." P. 12, l. 11, for "difapprove" r. "difprove." P. 15, l. 21, after "God" dele "and." P. 16, l. 1, for "duty" r. Deity." P. 17, l. 3, for "leaft" "r. left." P. 17, l. 28, dele "of." P. 18, l. 16, after "fill" infue "the," l. 28. for "into" r. "in." P. 20, l. ult. for "we" r. "it." P. 25, l. 9, for "offered" before "it" r. "offering." P. 26, l. 2, from the bottom, after "thofe" infue "who." P. 31, l. 12, for "infure" r. "enfue." P. 32, l. 27, for "fuckling" r. "fucking" P. 33, l. 10, before "kingdoms" dele "the." P. 38, l. 21, for "inculcated" r. "circulated." P. 45, l. 6, for "him" r. "man." P. 47, l. 11, for "was" r. "wax." P. 50, l. 2, from the bottom, for "commiffioners" r. "commiffions." P. 52, l. 3, before "give" infue "and," l. 7, for "thofe" r. "thou," l. 30, for "like fore" r. "fore like." P. 54, l. 2, for "which" r. "whom," l. 3, from the bottom, for "thefe" r. "there, l. 2, do. after "not with" enfue "you." P. 56, l. 23, before "has" infue "as."

www.ingramcontent.com/pod-product-compliance
Lightning Source LLC
Chambersburg PA
CBHW081522040426
42447CB00013B/3304